Transforming Behaviour

Transforming Behaviour
Pro-social modelling in practice

Sally Cherry

A HANDBOOK FOR PRACTITIONERS AND MANAGERS

WILLAN
PUBLISHING

Published by

Willan Publishing
Culmcott House
Mill Street, Uffculme
Cullompton, Devon
EX15 3AT, UK
Tel: +44(0)1884 840337
Fax: +44(0)1884 840251
e-mail: info@willanpublishing.co.uk
website: www.willanpublishing.co.uk

Published simultaneously in the USA and Canada by

Willan Publishing
c/o ISBS, 920 NE 58th Ave, Suite 300,
Portland, Oregon 97213-3786, USA
Tel: +001(0)503 287 3093
Fax: +001(0)503 280 8832
e-mail: info@isbs.com
website: www.isbs.com

First published 2005

ISBN 1-84392-166-9 paperback

British Library Cataloguing-in-Publication Data

A catalogue record for this book is available from the British Library

Project managed by Deer Park Productions, Tavistock, Devon
Typeset by GCS, Leighton Buzzard, Bedfordshire
Printed and bound by T.J. International, Padstow, Cornwall

Contents

Figures and tables

Acknowledgments

I wish to acknowledge the work of Chris Trotter, which has been a major influence on me in developing my thinking about pro-social modelling. When I contacted him to tell him I was writing this book his warm support was very much appreciated.

Many other people have helped me to develop my understanding of pro-social modelling in practice. First and foremost participants from many organisations, on many courses, who have participated enthusiastically and have openly shared their experience with me. Particular thanks go to the staff and managers of the eight hostels involved in the National Probation Directorate's Approved Pathfinder 2002–2004, who have been endlessly enthusiastic, open and welcoming; I have learned far more from them than I have taught them. Thanks also to Dave Brown and the staff of the Bethany Project, sadly now closed, where I cut my pro-social modelling teeth.

I have worked with many wise and experienced co-trainers when running pro-social modelling courses including Clare Cherry, Roger Clare, Catherine Fuller, Ian Hill, Gill Kelly, Phil Taylor, Louison Ricketts, and Bernadette Wilkinson. We have all shared in the development of thinking on this topic.

I want to thank friends and colleagues who have helped me by reading drafts of the various chapters, by helping me to think through various aspects of the topic and by keeping me going when I had failures of nerve. I also want to thank Peter Lewis who started me off on the pro-social path, Sarah Ackroyd, who was the catalyst for me getting down to writing, and Jane Allen, who gave me the title, ending a six-month long search. Special thanks go to Charlie Watson for all his help and support.

Many thanks go to Len Cheston; this would have been a lesser book without his careful reading and thoughtful comments. Rob Canton read a late draft and gave me pro-social and very helpful feedback which I really appreciated.

Finally I would like to thank my family Dick, Florence and Susanna, who are always there for me even when I am not pro-social.

Author's notes

A note on language

The majority of my experience is within the criminal justice system where we usually refer to our clients as 'offenders'. The language we use has important symbolic meaning and the term 'offender' is indicative of current thinking that says probation, prisons, etc., are part of the corrections system and exist to deal explicitly and unequivocally with offending behaviour and towards the cessation of that behaviour. The use of the term 'offender' can be criticised as labelling people and implying that they cannot change. Pro-social modelling is applicable outside the criminal justice system in any setting where practitioners are working with people they are trying to encourage to behave pro-socially; this might include school children, children looked after by the local authority, groups in the community, and young people within the youth justice system (where there is a heavy emphasis on prevention, as well as reduction, of criminal behaviour). So, in the quest for a relatively neutral term I use 'client' in this book, except where I am specifically using examples drawn from criminal justice.

The stories and case studies

All the stories in this book are based on real life examples, often those described by participants on courses. Apart from the account at the very beginning of the book which is reported exactly as it happened, names and situations have been changed in order to preserve anonymity. So, if you think you recognise your story in this book you might be right – but on the other hand you might not!

Foreword

by Dr Chris Trotter

It is with great pleasure that I write the foreword to *Transforming Behaviour: Pro-social Modelling in Practice*. Pro-social modelling has been demonstrated to be one of the key skills in effective work with offenders and other involuntary clients. The more we talk about it, the more we write about it and the more we learn about it, the greater the benefits will be for our clients, for direct practice workers and for the community. For this reason this book on pro-social practice is most welcome.

The book provides another perspective on pro-social modelling, an approach to work with involuntary clients developed in *Working with Involuntary Clients* and *Helping Abused Children and their Families*. It makes a real contribution to our knowledge about how to do pro-social practice which is defined broadly to incorporate a range of different techniques or models, including reflective listening, motivational interviewing, solution focused work and cognitive behavioural approaches.

The book includes numerous anecdotes and stories taken from the author's own experience in direct practice work with offenders and as a trainer. This helps to make the book enjoyable to read and grounded in the day to day work of probation officers and others in this field.

The book works through the various skills of empathy, use of authority, assertiveness, motivating the unwilling client, problem solving and being a pro-social manager. It also includes a number of exercises to help readers develop their skills in pro-social practice. Sally Cherry is a practitioner and trainer rather than an academic, nevertheless the book contains references to many of the research studies which support pro-social modelling.

I thoroughly recommend this book to anyone wishing to develop their skills in working with offenders and other involuntary clients.

Associate Professor
Monash University

'I have seen pro-social modelling transform the behaviour of staff and prisoners. Prison officers who learn to work pro-socially develop more rewarding and less tense relationships with prisoners. The prisoners who are treated pro-socially respond by behaving better, so everybody wins.'

Manager in a prison

1. Introduction

Listener serving a long sentence in a local prison: 'I tell people that if you need to you can talk to the prison officers too. Things have really changed here in the last few years. You really know now that staff are interested in you and they will listen to what you have to say.'

Visitor: 'How do you know that?'

Listener: 'They call you by your name and say "please" and "thank you" now.'

(Listeners are prisoners trained by the Samaritans to support other prisoners.)

This encounter is real – I was the visitor. I was taken to the First Night (induction) wing and invited to talk to anyone I wanted to. This is a Victorian prison, built for the containment and punishment of those whom many people wanted out of sight and out of mind. When I was a probation officer I could hardly bear to stay in the place long enough to interview a couple of people before I returned to freedom. The prison officers there still have to manage and control difficult people locked away in large groups; however, there has been a huge culture shift in the last few years.

What the Listener was describing to me was a simple example of pro-social modelling in practice. By treating the prisoners with respect the prison officers had gained the respect of this experienced prisoner.

There are many settings in which practitioners need to work constructively with people to help them to change their behaviour; this does not apply just to workers in the criminal justice system. All those who work with young people, i.e. teachers, youth workers, etc., are trying to help them grow up to be able to live successfully in society. In settings such as child protection, social workers are working to encourage major behaviour change in clients (or their families) who are frequently reluctant to change and resentful of the intervention. Doctors and other health workers are also often trying to influence patients' behaviour. Managers are trying to steer and develop their staff to be fully effective in their jobs. What they all have in common is that they are trying to uphold the values of the system they are working in ('crime is wrong', 'we need to respect others', 'smoking is bad for you', 'we do it this way here') while engaging constructively and ethically with the client, family, young person, patient or staff member.

Pro-social practice has many parallels with parenting in that it is about trying to steer someone in 'the right direction' by maintaining a caring relationship and being a positive role model. Just like parenting, it is much harder to do than to say, and although it often seems like common sense it is far from common practice. This book aims to give you support and guidance in developing your pro-social modelling in practice.

What are pro-social modelling and pro-social practice?

Pro-social modelling refers to the process by which the worker acts as a good motivating role model in order to bring out the best in people. The worker engages the client in an empathetic relationship within which they actively reinforce personal behaviour and attitudes and discourage anti-social behaviour and attitudes. Pro-social behaviour is not just the opposite of anti-social behaviour (including non-criminal behaviour); it also includes many of the other behaviours that make it possible for us to live together in society, such as being polite, being respectful, being punctual, apologising for mistakes, and so on.

Working pro-socially is ethical and respectful because it values clients as individuals and as members of society; it is optimistic about the possibility that the client can change and it seeks to engage the client as a partner in the change process. Pro-social modelling is popular with practitioners because it makes sense; it feels like the right way to behave, but it also gives them strategies to behave in this 'right way' both individually and as teams in their work with clients and one another. The other thing that makes it so appealing is that it is not just something that is 'done to' clients, it also describes the way in which staff can behave towards one another and managers should behave towards staff. It has the potential to transform the behaviour of both staff and clients.

Pro-social modelling has become a core element of work with offenders because it has been shown to be effective in helping to reduce offending. Chris Trotter is one of the best known researchers and writers in this field. In a study in Australia, Trotter (1999) demonstrated that after a consistent application of pro-social modelling, probation officers were half as likely to have clients who went to prison for breaching their orders. He also demonstrated that the approach works with young people and adults and with high-risk offenders and drug users. Understanding and practising pro-social modelling is not only useful in working with offenders (Trotter 1999 and 2004, also writes about abused children and their families) but also for working with anybody that we want to positively influence.

In every interaction with clients, practitioners have the opportunity to act as positive role models and to demonstrate formally and informally the behaviours and attitudes that they are encouraging in those clients; at its most basic this is what pro-social modelling is. Reminding practitioners of their importance as role models and helping them to identify just what they mean by pro-social modelling and how they use this formally and informally, as teams and as individuals, is a very important part of pro-social modelling training.

However, the term 'pro-social modelling' has come to describe something broader than just acting as a positive role model and is perhaps described more accurately as pro-social practice. This includes:

- Developing honest and empathetic relationships with clients, which demonstrate a genuine concern for the person, and persistence and optimism about their capacity to change.

- Modelling and encouraging pro-social behaviour. This includes being clear with oneself and one's team about underlying values, and clear with the client about expectations of values and behaviour and using rewards to reinforce these.

- Discouraging by challenging and confronting undesired values and behaviour, including the discouragement of pro-criminal and anti-social values and behaviour.

- The transparent, clear, and appropriate use of authority, and the role of enforcement (often described as legitimacy).

- Clarity and openness about the role of staff and the purpose and expectations of any interventions.

- Actively working in partnership with clients to help them to change by increasing their motivation, coaching them in new skills, clear objective setting, planned and negotiated problem solving and the monitoring of progress.

- Treating the client as an individual and valuing their differences and similarities to others. This includes avoiding stereotyping and valuing diversity of ethnicity, cultural experience, gender, sexuality, differing abilities, etc. Also working at an appropriate level for the client's speaking and listening abilities, and working with different thinking and learning styles.

This list, which is developed from Kemshall and Canton *et al.* (2003), demonstrates that pro-social modelling is both a way of thinking and behaving and a series of strategies.

In this book the term pro-social practice is used to describe the wide range of activities that need to be undertaken for effective pro-social modelling.

The purpose of this book

There are ever increasing amounts of first stage training available on pro-social modelling (see details on page 178). However, experience as a trainer and consultant in this field shows me that although people leave courses enthused and committed to working pro-socially, this is much harder to do in practice than in theory. This is especially the case if the whole team has not been trained and/or their managers are not well versed and active in modelling and reinforcing pro-social work. In this case pro-social practice often rapidly becomes diluted.

The book is intended as an accessible guide to what pro-social practice is and how to do it. It contains straightforward 'how to do it' explanations. It is not enough in today's 'evidence-based' environment to do things just because they seem like a good idea, so the book refers to the evidence base. There is much written about theory but remarkably little about practice so I have tried to read the available material and relate it to practice. Any errors of interpretation are entirely my own. In the Further Reading section I recommend some books that do link theory and practice that I have found particularly useful.

I am not an academic, so my developing understanding of pro-social practice has been through discussion with the hundreds of practitioners and managers that I have met when facilitating training and consultancy. Many of their stories are in here in one form or another, as well as some answers to the many questions I have been asked.

The structure of the book

In writing this book I have in mind the busy practitioner who may not have time to read it as a whole. The Contents page lists in detail what is in each chapter and each chapter also has a short summary at the end. The remainder of this Introduction introduces the reader to more of the theoretical support for pro-social practice. This is a practitioner's book so

I have tried to give you enough theory so that you feel confident that there is an evidence base but not enough to overwhelm you. There is a full list of references at the back of the book if you want to follow up the theory in more detail.

Underpinning all pro-social practice is engaging with the client in an empathetic relationship. There are specific practitioner skills which allow us to do this, such as listening, asking questions and reflecting what the client has said and meant. It is to be hoped that all practitioners in the 'people business' have some interpersonal skills and indeed many have excellent skills. However, this is an endlessly fascinating subject where there is always something new to learn and **Chapter 2: Developing empathetic relationships and working in a solution-focused way** addresses this topic; it also helps you to develop optimistic and solution-focused practice.

Pro-social modelling is underpinned by clear values. While retaining respectful and empathetic relationships with clients, practitioners are trying to steer them towards an explicit point of view and particular kinds of behaviour. Research (Bottoms and Rex 1998; Rex and Crosland 1999) has demonstrated that the legitimate use of authority is one of the most important aspects of pro-social modelling. **Chapter 3: Exploring the legitimate use of authority: roles, rules, values, expectations and rewards** helps you to be clear about the values underpinning your practice and how these are translated into work with clients, by thinking about the behaviour you are seeking to encourage (and discourage) and how you positively reward desired behaviour. When working with a value set that is not simply client-centred, the most effective way to maintain an open and honest relationship is to be very clear about roles and also to ensure that the use of power is transparent and appropriate. This chapter gives you guidelines for this.

It is one thing to have a clear idea about what you want clients to do, it is often much more difficult to actually steer them in that direction by clearly telling them what you like and dislike about their behaviour. It is particularly hard to do this in a way that does not sound like lecturing and that the client actually hears and listens to. **Chapter 4: Assertive interactions and pro-social feedback** introduces and explains simple assertiveness techniques and then gives guidelines for using these to give pro-social feedback. Like most of the techniques in this book this is as applicable to working with colleagues as it is to working with clients.

Clients may not want to change and practitioners can increase their motivation by using specific techniques, such as motivational interviewing of which the best known proponents are Miller and Rollnick (1991, 2002). It is a client-centred technique yet it is used in settings such as criminal justice to motivate the client to change according to the practitioner's definition rather than the client's definition of what the desirable change might be. There is some debate among practitioners about how motivational work and pro-social modelling work together: **Chapter 5: Motivating the unwilling client** looks both at motivational techniques and at how motivational work and pro-social modelling can be integrated in practice.

Even when they want to change, clients often do not because they do not know how or because they are anxious and scared. **Chapter 6: Practical ways of helping people to change** gives guidance on how to teach new skills using a simple step-by-step model.

Chapter 7: Taking a systematic, pro-social, collaborative approach to problem solving pulls all the threads of the previous chapters together and gives you guidelines for planning and monitoring interventions over a period of time. It also guides you in techniques for engaging clients as partners in their own change process by being clear and transparent about goal setting, objective setting and problem solving.

While we might see offending and other anti-social behaviour as a problem for society, offenders and others behaving anti-socially often see their behaviour as a response to a problem (such as racism, poverty, lack of opportunity, etc.). At the heart of pro-social practice is the working relationship that is formed with the client. So while we should be aiming to work with clients in a way which is consistent and coherent from one to the other, we also need to treat everyone as individuals. **Chapter 8: Responding to individual need and diversity** looks at how responding to diverse individuals is far more than having some knowledge of different groups of people; it is about being willing to learn and develop our thinking. It also discusses some specific differences and similarities among clients that we need to take account of and respond to.

Pro-social modelling is at its most powerful and effective when it is a whole organisation activity and when it is constantly reinforced by and supported by managers. **Chapter 9: Being a pro-social manager: becoming a pro-social organisation** contains help for managers in becoming a pro-social manager. It also includes some ideas for embedding and reinforcing pro-social modelling in teams and in the wider organisation.

At the end of the book are **Appendices A–E** containing exercises that I have found useful for developing and embedding pro-social modelling with teams. These are not intended to replace a good introductory training programme but could be used by managers to keep pro-social modelling on the boil over a period of time.

The evidence base for pro-social modelling

Work with offenders, and other people, is incredibly complex. Many factors come into play of which the relationship with a practitioner and/

or organisation is only one. The debate about what works is ongoing and is unlikely to ever achieve definitive answers because the debate itself shifts ground according to political and social influences. However, there is a consistent thread that runs through much of the research that refers to the importance of the relationship between worker and client, and the purposeful and reflective use of this relationship as a positive influence on the client.

The term pro-social modelling and the concept of working pro-socially have gained currency steadily in the UK since being brought to our notice in the early 1990s by Chris Trotter (1994), who in turn was developing the work of Don Andrews. In research studies they both demonstrated that supervision which is based on developing a close working relationship between the client and the worker, and looking out for and reinforcing pro-social behaviours and expression, are associated with reduced reoffending (see, for example, Trotter 1999; Dowden and Andrews 2004).

As long ago as 1971 Sinclair (1971) showed that hostel regimes where staff were 'firm but kindly' and who were supportive but clear about the rules (although this was not called pro-social modelling this is what he is effectively describing) had a significant influence on reconviction rates in the short term, although these effects generally did not continue beyond the period of residence.

There have been several subsequent studies including:

- Research into the implementation of pro-social modelling in Approved Premises (Probation Service Hostels) in West Yorkshire (Loney *et al.* 2000). This approach was associated with improved staff–resident and staff–staff relationships and improved positive feedback and constructive criticism by staff in their relationships with residents.

- Research into the implementation of pro-social modelling in Approved Premises in South Yorkshire (Henry *et al.* 2000), which reported increased job satisfaction among staff and a significant improvement in the behaviour of hostel residents.

- Research by Gill McIvor (1998) into pro-social modelling in Community Service in Scotland which demonstrated that the quality of the offender's experience (a positive experience being one based on consistency, fairness and mutual respect) had a direct impact on levels of compliance.

- Research by Bottoms and Rex (1998: 19), who suggest that 'probationers want probation to be a purposeful experience, appreciate probation officers who show respect and concern for them and are more ready to accept a certain amount of encouragement and direction from supervisors who do so'.

- Research into seven Community Service Pathfinders (pilots) (Rex *et al.* 2004) which suggests that projects focusing on skills accreditation and pro-social modelling were promising.

- A meta-analysis (a review of a number of research studies) by Dowden and Andrews (2004) that takes as its starting point five dimensions of correctional practice:

  - The firm but fair use of authority.
  - Modelling pro-social and anti-criminal attitudes, cognition and behaviours.
  - Teaching concrete problem solving skills.
  - Using community resources (brokerage).
  - Forming and working through warm, open and enthusiastic relationships.

Dowden and Andrews found that the greater the number of indicators of core correctional practice the greater the reduction in offending. In other words they found that the quality of interactions with staff and the degree to which they model pro-social behaviour are critical to the aim of reducing reoffending.

Pro-social modelling also parallels other work including that on positive parenting. Parenting (on a good day) involves encouraging children to do more of the things that you, the parent, think will help them grow into decent people and citizens, and discouraging them from doing things that you think are anti-social. It also involves behaving in ways that you want your children to emulate because if you do not you can be sure they will reproduce your bad behaviour, usually at the most inappropriate time. This is all done in a loving, accepting environment with the clearest of rules and boundaries. Substituting the word 'empathetic' for 'loving' describes pro-social modelling.

In the field of criminal justice in particular, pro-social modelling is becoming central to much practice. For instance the recently published Offender Management model for the National Offender Management Service states that the NOMS Model is built around an **offender-focused human services approach** (2005: 4: original emphasis). The paper goes on to describe the importance of core correctional practice (based on Dowden and Andrews 2004).

Quite apart from the fact that studies show that pro-social practice works, part of its appeal is that it puts the one-to-one client–worker relationship back at the heart of work with offenders, at a time when often the practitioner feels more like a broker of services and enforcer of rules.

Pro-social practice is often criticised as being what people are doing anyway and is nothing new. It is what people should be doing, but one of the problems with pro-social practice is identifying what it really is and then consistently implementing it. Research by Bonta and Rugge (2004) in Canada found that corrections officers frequently did not actually address issues with the client that were related to their offending behaviour. They also found that while corrections officers were quite good at rewarding or affirming pro-social expressions and behaviours they often failed to respond to anti-social behaviours or expressions.

Pro-social modelling is not about being nice to people. It is about using a warm and empathetic relationship purposefully to encourage more pro-social behaviour and discourage anti-social behaviour. If the corrections officer were not addressing criminal behaviour (the reason why the client was a client) they could not be doing this.

Pro-social practice is not a magic bullet. Clients have many complex problems that cannot be solved just by encouraging pro-social behaviour. However, a pro-social working relationship can be the vehicle through which clients are helped to tackle practical problems and learn different behaviours.

I have been asked whether pro-social work is suitable for mentally disordered people. The term 'mentally disordered' covers a huge range and number of people. Kemshall (2004a) suggests that in 2003 27 per cent of probation clients were defined by their supervising officers as having some form of mental disorder. I am not aware of any research on pro-social practice with mentally disordered clients specifically; however, Laurance (2003), in his highly critical account of services for the mentally ill in Britain, states that the services are failing patients because they use physical and chemical containment rather than engaging and motivating patients to be partners in their own care. I have recently had discussions with the manager of a hostel for mentally disordered offenders and a social worker working in a prison with severely mentally disordered people including psychopaths. Both these discussions lead me to believe that pro-social practice, with its emphasis on firm and fair implementation of rules and boundaries, responsiveness to the individual and consistent modelling of desirable behaviour, supported by strategies for helping people to change, is likely to be very helpful in such work.

The worker as a role model

One of the principal ways in which we learn new behaviours is by observing other people. Social learning theory (Bandura 1977) demonstrated that learning can take place through observation without the learners themselves being involved in, or directly suffering any consequences from, the behaviour. Learning is more likely to take place if the activity being modelled is one that the learner thinks is important and the person doing the modelling has the respect of the observer. In a report on the implementation of the National Offender Management Model Pathfinder in the North West, an offender was quoted as saying: 'I want to be as helpful to the probation service as they have been helpful to me' (PA and Mori 2005: 26).

Anti-social behaviour is often learned from others and reinforced by others; for instance experience, supported by research, shows us the importance of peer groups in influencing young people into behaviour that they would be very unlikely to undertake on their own. Huesmann and Podolski (2004) describe how children learn aggressive behaviour from observing others acting aggressively, and how they can develop the tendency to see hostility where there is none from viewing a lot of violence.

Positive role models are equally important. In many work settings, especially where there is an opportunity for a high 'dosage' of worker–client contact such as youth clubs, prisons, residential premises, etc., the clients have many opportunities to observe how the workers interact with them, with other clients and with one another. Therefore it is very important the workers ensure that they model appropriate behaviour and attitudes as often as possible.

Fortunately pro-social modelling is a forgiving model as it recognises that workers cannot be perfect all the time. Two very useful skills are finding strategies for retrieving a situation after making a mistake and apologising. A lot of offending and other inappropriate behaviour follows on from a mistake or a situation that could have been retrievable. Therefore if you do not get something right and the client notices, this is an opportunity to model dealing with mistakes. For instance, publicly acknowledging when you have made a mistake and apologising can be a really powerful piece of modelling for clients to learn from.

> Marianne is the manager of a probation hostel. Arriving at work early and thinking that she was alone, she was having a cigarette leaning out of the office window while reading the notes in the handover book from the day before. Cara, one of the residents who was setting off to work, spotted her. 'I thought that smoking wasn't allowed in the office,' said Cara. 'What is this, one rule for you and one rule for us?'
>
> 'You are right,' said Marianne, putting out her cigarette. 'I should not have done that, the no-smoking rule applies to everyone including me ... I'm sorry.'

Behaviours that workers need to demonstrate in order to be a positive role model are those which they want to see in the client and include:

- **Respect for the individual**: I am genuinely interested in you and I want to try and understand your point of view.

- **Respect for the law and for rules**

- **Punctuality**

- **Reliability**: I will do what I said I would do unless there is a very good reason not to, and if this is the case I will explain why I have not done it.

- **Consistency**: I will try to treat you the same over time and also treat others the same from one to another as far as I can, bearing in mind their individual needs.

- **Fairness**: I will try to treat you according to your needs and not make unreasonable demands.

- **Putting things right**: If I make a mistake I will say so, put it right and apologise.

- **Assertiveness**: In my interactions with others I will aim for a win, I will be clear about what I am thinking and feeling and want to happen, but also try to understand what you are thinking and feeling and what you want to happen.

Trotter's research (2004: 127) demonstrated that client outcomes were better when workers kept appointments and responded to phone calls promptly. Client outcomes were particularly poor when workers were repeatedly late. The study suggested that 'what might be described as simple courtesies are just as important or even more important than other direct practice skills such as working through problems'.

Optimum conditions for modelling

There are factors that are more likely to make a role model credible and effective. The following list is adapted from Gast and Taylor (1998):

- The ideal model is someone who is respected and has credibility in the eyes of the client. One of the ways in which the worker gains this credibility is to be seen over a period of time to be fair, transparent about the rules and consistent in the implementation of them (see discussion of legitimacy in Chapter 3).

- The role model needs to have a degree of confidence and fluency in what they are modelling. They need to ensure that they are not demonstrating excessive anxiety or embarrassment, for instance.

- The modelling is likely to be more credible if the worker is not too perfect. When someone does something without any apparent effort that you find hard to do yourself, the situation can seem very intimidating. However, if the modelling includes trying hard to achieve a goal, dealing with setbacks and mistakes, the client is much more likely to be prepared to have a go.

- It is important to remember that not everyone thinks or learns in the same way (see Chapter 8).

- In a group setting, such as a hostel, a school or a club, it may be the case that other people are modelling very different behaviour but have a powerful influence on the client. The worker may need to take account of this. For instance, most teenagers will behave very differently with their peers than they would on their own with an adult. A youth worker who wants to have a serious conversation with one member is much more likely to be able to influence that person if they conduct the conversation away from the rest of the group.

Becoming more pro-social: growing up sooner or later?

Lunness (2000) describes the theory underpinning a social and moral reasoning programme which helps young people develop more mature thinking processes. Immaturity as described below is not the prerogative of young people and I include this because it is helpful to understand some of the processes we take a client through when trying to help them to develop more pro-social thinking.

Immature behaviour is often associated with anti-social behaviour. In psychological terms this immature type of thinking is often characterised as (Lunness 2000: 9):

- **Egocentric**: thinking about yourself, not considering others.

- **Externally controlled**: any motivation to behave in pro-social ways comes from a desire to avoid punishment or detection.

- **Concrete**: thinking about the particular situation, not able to see beyond to more general principles, such as ideas of justice or responsibilities towards others.

- **Instrumental**: behaviour is justified as a direct exchange with others, e.g. someone steals your bike, so you steal another; 'it's all right if someone does it to you'.

- **Impulsive**: acting on the needs of the moment, often illogically.

- **Short-term**: acting without considering longer-term consequences.

Often the client displaying anti-social behaviour has difficulty in putting themselves in others' shoes, to imagine how a victim might be affected or to be aware of the effects on wider society.

The more mature stages which are associated with more pro-social or law abiding behaviour are characterised by Lunness (2000: 9) as follows:

- **Sociocentric**: awareness of others, both as individuals and as members of a community and society.

- **Internally controlled**: actions are guided by thought about the consequences, including longer-term effects, and how others will be affected as well as self.

- **Empathic**: able to see things from another's point of view, e.g. how someone else would feel as the victim of crime.

- **Pro-social**: valuing personal relationships for their own sake and appreciating of the benefits of social order and values more generally.

The more mature individual is able to appreciate the consequences of behaviour to themselves and others in the short and longer term. Therefore their motivation to behave in socially constructive ways is not simply to avoid sanctions.

Lunness suggests that many young offenders have been shown to operate at the early stage of moral development. They are not equipped to deal with difficulties such as personal relationships or conflict. Often their reaction to a difficulty makes matters worse rather than better. Many of these characteristics often appear to be a factor in adult offending and other anti-social behaviour too.

The failure to progress to more mature stages is not necessarily associated with a lack of intellectual ability but is more likely to be due to a lack of opportunities to learn, including a lack of role models. Much of the work with offenders is focused on enabling them to develop the cognitive skills necessary to behave in a more mature way. However, this model also gives us clues as to the kind of behaviour and thinking that we need to be modelling to clients if we are going to influence them towards more mature and pro-social behaviour.

Organisational modelling

One of the reasons that pro-social practice is so powerful is that it is not just something that workers do with (or to) clients but it operates at all levels within an organisation. The kind of pro-social behaviours and expressions that we want to encourage in clients, such as consideration of others, expressing anti-crime views, listening to our point of view, are very similar if not the same as those we want to encourage in our colleagues, our managers and those whom we manage.

Pro-social modelling is for all staff and involves managers modelling to staff, colleagues modelling to one another, staff modelling to clients and clients being helped to behave pro-socially to one another.

Pro-social practice is about all aspects of the organisation's work and should be mirrored in organisational policies, procedures, decision making and the working of committees, management teams and staff supervision.

Organisational behaviour enables or inhibits pro-social behaviour by providing examples for staff, structures that support pro-social activity and support and skill development for staff.

An organisation commissioned a series of training courses in pro-social modelling for its staff. When the training started there were all sorts of problems. Training was held on site in rooms, usually the TV room, that were not suitable for training, they were too small, and furnished with sofas and squashy chairs. The service users had not been told that the TV room was being used so, not unreasonably, they kept knocking on the door. Lunch was not always provided; staff had received joining instructions very late or not at all. Very few managers came to the training.

The message that the staff heard was very clear. 'We have not committed ourselves wholeheartedly to this training; also we do not care enough about you to ensure you have a decent experience on this course.'

Despite all this, some of the staff embraced the training enthusiastically but it was unlikely that they would be able to make an impact in such an unsympathetic environment.

(See Chapter 9 for further discussion of organisational modelling.)

Parallel processes: ensuring that the influence is in the right direction

The concept of parallel processes has its origin in the psychoanalytical concepts of transference and counter-transference. It was first recognised in the supervision of professional practice of therapists, when the therapist recreated the presenting problem and emotions of the therapist–client relationship within the supervisory relationship and then the supervisor responded to the therapist in a similar manner. Thus the supervisory interaction replays or is parallel with the counselling interaction (Sumerel 1994). It was also recognised in work with divorcing parents that was often undertaken by pairs of workers, there was a real risk that the pairs of workers would start to play out the same dynamics between themselves as the conflicting couple were playing out in interviews.

Parallel processes can also take place in organisations and there is a risk that staff will start mirroring some of the problematic behaviours of the clients, and vice versa. We need to ensure that the direction of influence is positive and supports pro-social behaviour.

In practice this means that staff need to endeavour to behave pro-socially towards one another all the time and managers need to be constantly reinforcing this in supervision and in informal interactions. This is not always easy. In the research in South Yorkshire hostels, staff complained that they felt that they were always being watched (and watching themselves). However, they also reported that training in pro-social modelling helped them to step back and criticise their own behaviour, it gave them an enhanced sense of job satisfaction and was self-rewarding and self-reinforcing (Henry *et al.* 2000).

Staff in residential settings such as hostels and prisons often report that there are times when the atmosphere feels very tense and they cannot always put their finger on why this is. They say that this spreads to the staff team and they become irritable and tense too. However, if they realise what is happening and all make a conscious effort to be calm with one another and clients, the tension often subsides.

Teams and individuals that I have worked with have developed a set of 'pro-social filters' that warn them when their behaviour is less than pro-social. Sometimes I have heard them say (not in front of their clients) 'I am going to be un-pro-social for minute' before having a good rant and then getting on with the job. To me this is a sign that they are very conscious of their own behaviour but also of being normal fallible human beings.

In one hostel, although there has been no conscious effort to teach them the meaning of the word, the residents talk about what is and is not pro-social behaviour including teasing the staff about some of their behaviour not being pro-social. I take this to be a sign that the staff are influencing the residents and that pro-social modelling is firmly embedded in the organisation.

Cognitive Behavioural Theory

Cognitive Behavioural Theory is the theoretical basis of many of the current interventions with offenders, and pro-social modelling can be related theoretically to the family of cognitive behavioural interventions. Cognitive behaviourism represents a synthesis between different psychological approaches, behaviourism (focused on observable behaviour) and cognitivism (focused on cognitions or subjectivity). The theoretical model recognises an inter-relationship between thoughts, feelings and behaviour. There is an interaction between the individual's internal world and the external environment and behaviour is seen as a product of the interplay between personal–internal and situational–external factors (McGuire 2000).

Thinking (cognition) is conceptualised as a complex developmental process, during which a person develops a greater or lesser ability to control and understand the relationship between their thoughts, feelings and behaviour in relation to external and internal factors and consequently to regulate their behaviour appropriately (appropriate behaviour being defined by such things as rules, laws, social norms). However, because cognitive abilities are learned rather than innate there is the possibility of developing new learning that enables the subject to change their behaviour.

Cognitive Behavioural Theory is sometimes depicted diagrammatically by an iceberg where the tip of the iceberg is the actions or behaviour that we can see and under the water are the thoughts and feelings that we can only infer from behaviour, including self-report.

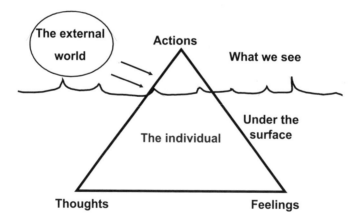

Figure 1.1 The cognitive behavioural iceberg

Cognitive behavioural interventions have their critics (see, for example, Mair 2004). They are criticised for being propounded as a panacea for all ills and for being simplistic and focusing on the individual and their responsibility to change rather than the complexity of environmental and other factors that also impinge on them. However, as McGuire (2000) says, it is not suggested that this approach or the methods based on it have all the answers. There are still many questions to be answered, and room for many innovations and developments. Cognitive behavioural interventions have become so influential in many fields that it important to have at least a basic acquaintance with the theory.

Although pro-social modelling has different theoretical roots it is congruent with the family of cognitive behavioural interventions. A complex emotional and behavioural dynamic exists between workers and clients and diagrammatically pro-social practice can be explained in terms of the cognitive behavioural iceberg (Figure 1.2).

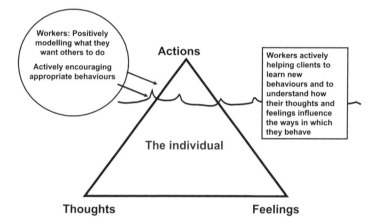

Figure 1.2   The cognitive behavioural iceberg: pro-social practice

How the cognitive behavioural iceberg helps the practitioner

Apart from giving the practitioner a theoretical understanding, the model – and specifically the concept of the iceberg where behaviour is on view and thoughts and feelings are hidden (under the water) – has a very practical application for the practitioner. When trying to understand behaviour and therefore get an insight into how to encourage people to change their behaviour it is always useful to ask what is going on under the water? In other words, what are the thoughts and feelings that are leading to this behaviour?

Janet had been working with a team over a period of time developing a new piece of work. She had met all the team members and got on well with them. On a return visit she found herself faced by a group of people who could only be described as sullen. Something was clearly not right but she had no idea what. She did not know whether something had happened in the team, or whether it was a problem with the day and/or with her. Janet had received feedback from the team's manager that the new project was going well but when she asked the team about it she received a stream of negative comments.

To cut a long story short, it turned out that several of the team had come in outside their shift time, they were not really sure what the day was for, there had been a lot of 'checking up' in the form of quality assurance systems, and they were not sure whether Janet had come to check up on them or help them. Some of them were also feeling a great deal of insecurity about the skills they needed for the new project and felt that this had not been acknowledged.

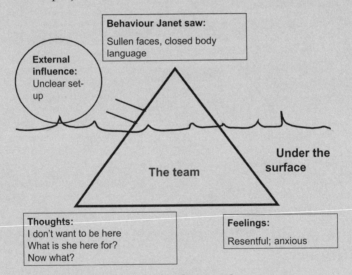

Figure 1.3 What is going on under the water?

Their cognitive behavioural iceberg looked something like Figure 1.3. Fortunately Janet realised quickly that something was not right. She knew the group quite well and had credibility with them. She reflected to the group that she felt something was not right and they responded by expressing some of their anxieties. She quickly began to understand the thoughts and feelings that were leading to the behaviour and addressed these. She explained that she was there to help and not to check up. She acknowledged some of the group members' anxiety about whether they had the necessary skills and reassured them that part of the day would be spent on skills development. As soon as these things had been addressed, the behaviour of the group members changed, they became more open and relaxed and the day progressed successfully.

This example refers to a group of people but the iceberg is equally useful for understanding individual behaviour.

Pro-social practice in a variety of settings

Most of my experience is in criminal justice settings – I was a probation officer. I am now a trainer and consultant working with a variety of organisations including probation, prisons, youth justice and voluntary sector bodies working with offenders. Most of the research on pro-social work also refers to criminal justice settings. However, it is my belief that the principles of pro-social practice – the importance of an empathetic relationship between client and worker, the importance of the worker as a role model, the importance of being clear about rules and implementing them fairly – are applicable to many professional and other settings even though it may go by another name.

Examples include:

- **Education**: Teachers are on show constantly to their pupils and young people do not miss much. For instance, my children know exactly which teachers smoke. They also prefer teachers who are firm but fair to those who are inconsistent in mood and behaviour. More formally, positive behaviour management strategies and anti-bullying policies are underpinned by pro-social principles such as being clear what the rules are and implementing them quickly when necessary, and expecting older children to act as role models for younger children.

- **Youth work**: Similar principles apply to youth work; however, the setting is likely to be more informal. This means that youth workers have to work even harder to harness the positive influences among young people and to be a positive influence themselves.

- **Social work**: The term covers a variety of activities but again the worker is often trying to help people to behave differently by actively discouraging unhelpful behaviour and encouraging more appropriate behaviour. Child protection is one aspect of social work. For more information about using a pro-social approach in child protection see Trotter (2004). Understanding pro-social practice is particularly relevant when the social worker is acting in *loco parentis*, for instance, with looked-after children, fostering and remand fostering.

- **Healthcare**: A lot of health care work is aimed at persuading the patients to take care of their own health. This message is undermined if the professional does not build a rapport with the patients well enough to communicate with them and/or is manifestly not looking after their own health (for instance, is very overweight or smells of cigarettes).

- **Management**: See Chapter 9.

- **Parenting**: Parenting at its best is about teaching young people all the skills, behaviours and attitudes that they need to live successfully in society. It is about teaching children the rules and encouraging them to keep these while valuing and celebrating the child's individuality. All this takes place within a loving environment where, although the child may rebel at times, overall they have enough respect and regard for the parent to want to please them and sometimes copy them. The ultimate aim of a parent is to do oneself out of a job as the child grows up and is able to manage their own life.

We have already seen that pro-social behaviour is associated with psychological maturity. Pro-social modelling can be seen as parenting for grown-ups not in the sense that clients are treated like children, but in the sense that within a caring and appropriate relationship the client feels respected and valued and learns appropriate patterns of behaviour by copying the worker. Also the client is encouraged to stop some behaviours and helped to learn some other new and more helpful behaviours. Often, in terms of helping the client to learn to live as a law-abiding member of society, the worker is doing what, for one reason or another, the client's parents were unable to do.

Summary

Pro-social behaviour is the behaviour that makes it possible for us to live together in society, such as being law abiding, polite, respectful, apologising for mistakes, and so on.

The aim of much work with many different kinds of clients is to encourage them towards a more pro-social lifestyle.

The model is underpinned by a very clear set of values that the client may or may not subscribe to, but it is also client-focused and solution-focused and is responsive to them as an individual.

Practitioners like pro-social practice because it is ethical, people-centred and it makes common sense.

There is also an increasing body of research that demonstrates that pro-social practice is effective practice.

Pro-social practice equips the worker to be a positive role model and to actively encourage more pro-social behaviour and less anti-social behaviour.

Pro-social practice is not just something we do with (or to) clients; it is an activity for the whole organisation.

Pro-social practice relates theoretically to the family of cognitive behavioural interventions.

Understanding the thoughts and feelings that underpin people's behaviour is useful for workers and for clients.

Pro-social practice is useful in a variety of settings including criminal justice, education, youth work, social work, healthcare and management.

Pro-social practice can be described as parenting for grown-ups.

2. Developing empathetic relationships and working in a solution-focused way

'I always thought that I was a good listener, but in reality all I did was say "what I would do if I were you is this ..." Since I learned about pro-social modelling I really listen and try to understand what the young person is really talking about.' (Youth worker)

Introduction

Our ability to be a pro-social influence is underpinned by our ability to form positive and appropriate relationships with clients. We are aiming to influence and steer them towards behaviours and attitudes that we think are pro-social while genuinely trying to understand the world from their point of view. But how do we do this, how do we achieve empathy with people some of whom will have poor interpersonal skills and some of whom inhabit a world that we may find abhorrent?

This chapter addresses this question and looks at the endlessly fascinating subject of effective interpersonal skills. Trotter (2004) describes a study looking at child protection workers which demonstrated that training for workers in listening and counselling skills has a positive effect on client outcomes, and that when clients believed that the worker tried to understand their point of view, the outcomes were better.

This chapter also gives guidance for working in an optimistic and solution-focused way, which has been shown by Trotter (1999) to be very important in increasing the likelihood that the worker will be an influence for positive change.

The meaning of your behaviour is in the way in which it is received

Achieving empathy means attempting to put yourself in another's shoes, to imagine the world from their point of view. However, it is not enough for us to know that we are trying to understand the client's point of view; they need to know too. Interpersonal communications are like a dance, with each partner responding to the other's moves and adjusting their responses accordingly. When engaging with unwilling and/or difficult clients the practitioner's interpersonal skills must be very finely honed, as (returning to the analogy of the dance) his or her partner in the interaction may be unskilled or clumsy.

Dave was a lonely young man. Brought up in care and then spending time in prison as a young man he had few opportunities to develop relationships with women, even though he longed to. On release from prison he moved to a probation hostel where Sandy was allocated as his key worker. She was genuinely interested in Dave and could see his potential to settle down and become law-abiding. She worked hard to get to know him and to work out ways in which he could be supported through the process of adjustment to living in society. However, she soon became aware that Dave was beginning to behave as if theirs was a personal rather than a professional relationship. Dave's desperation for a close relationship and his lack of social experience had led him to misread her interactions with him even though she had always behaved appropriately.

Fortunately Sandy was sufficiently skilled to see this happening at a very early stage and to adjust her behaviour so that she was slightly more distant. She also opened up some discussion with Dave about relationships which made it very clear to him that sooner or later she was expecting him to have relationships with women he met outside of the hostel, and, by implication, that there was absolutely no thought in her mind of her relationship with him straying into a personal one.

Not everyone is like me

One of the key threads running through this chapter and the rest of the book is 'not everyone is like me (or you)'. In this context it is important to remember that not everyone communicates like me and not everyone will interpret things the way I do. This applies to every aspect of communication, from cross-cultural differences to the meaning we ascribe to someone else smiling at us. The only way we are ever going to come near to understanding what other people mean is to keep picking up, reflecting and testing the meaning of their communications.

Empathising not colluding

It is important to remember that empathising with people does not mean colluding with them or in any way necessarily showing approval of their actions. Neither does it mean just being nice. It is possible to achieve empathy with people without conveying the message that you agree with what they do or have done. This is a tightrope that people working with offenders and/or other clients who have undertaken anti-social actions have to walk every day. Trotter (1999) quotes research that shows that probation workers who simply empathised with offenders (the research measured levels of empathy by analysing the nature of interactions) did not increase the chances of the offender behaving pro-socially and reducing reoffending. In fact, in some cases, the clients increased offending. The assumption is that by appearing to be understanding, the worker inadvertently conveyed the message that they understood the offending and even thought that it was all right. However, where the probation workers combined empathy with pro-social reinforcement, in other words they encouraged pro-social behaviour and discouraged anti-social behaviour, this led to reduced offending.

It appears that getting into a empathetic relationship with clients opens the door to influencing them. However, if we do not make pro-social values and expectations clear and explicit it is possible to influence clients in undesirable as well as desirable directions. Chapter 3 discusses pro-social values and how these are manifested and reinforced in practice. In all interactions it is important to be clear when behaviour described and/or views expressed are not pro-social but to do this in a way which signifies acceptance of the person or at least an attempt to try and understand the person's motives, i.e. 'I can see that you had no money for drugs and that you were desperate but that does not make it OK to steal from other people' (this in the context of a longer discussion where rapport is established).

Sometimes it is very difficult to understand someone's motives and indeed you may not want to even try (in the case of sex offenders, for instance). In this case the best that you might be able to do is signal that you are prepared to go on working with them, that you see them as more than the sum of their offences and demonstrate some optimism that they can change while being honest that you cannot understand their motivation, i.e. 'So you are saying that it was not hurting anyone looking at photos on the internet and you would never actually touch a child. I understand what you are saying and I believe that you would never deliberately hurt a child. However, I don't agree that photos are harmless: how do you think they were taken?'

Active and reflective listening

Active and reflective listening is both the means by which you get into empathy with someone and the means by which you demonstrate to them that you are in empathy with them. These are skills that we need for everyday interactions, not just in a more structured relationship such as between case manager or key worker and client.

Active and reflective listening means listening and responding not only to the words spoken but the meanings behind them, and to all the subtle unspoken signs. Research by Albert Menrabhain (1972) demonstrated that words form only 7 per cent of the total message that we convey; 55 per cent of the meaning is in signals that we give with our bodies, and 38 per cent with our voice. Peter Collet (2004) gives numerous examples of the subtle ways in which our body language demonstrates what we are really thinking and feeling: he calls these 'tells'. For example, someone who is feeling anxious in a situation may demonstrate a range of tells, many of which are linked to the suppressed urge to flee. These might include foot-tapping, sudden and jerky hand movement, and rapid and shallow breath.

What happens to the other person when we do not listen?

Sometimes people are aware that they are not being listened to and they respond accordingly. We have all been in this situation, for instance, in a coffee bar, trying to talk to a friend who is 'people watching' over your shoulder. In this case you will probably feel able to be quite assertive and draw your friend's attention back to yourself. If they continue to be distracted you might get angry, but you would be aware that other person was not listening.

Often when people feel that they are not being listened to they report that they feel undervalued or boring and do not recognise that it is the listener whose behaviour is causing that feeling. In other words, they perceive the situation as being due to some lack in themselves not in the listener. These feelings are often reflected in their speech: 'I know this story isn't very interesting' or 'I know that I am boring'. People who have a low sense of their own self-worth are particularly vulnerable to feeling undervalued. Not being listened to can lead to a sense of frustration, which can in turn lead to inappropriate behaviour, such as aggression. This is the kind of situation that we should try to avoid.

Good listening is a collection of behaviours used to build rapport with others; it is an interaction, a two-way process, and we are doing it all the time. Some of the clients we work with may not have learned very effective interpersonal skills or they may be stressed or angry, which makes it much harder to develop a rapport, so we have to work harder and more consciously at getting it right.

Skills for active and reflective listening

Eye contact

On training courses, when asked 'what is a sign of active listening?' the first thing people usually say is eye contact. Sometimes they even come out with suggestions such as 'you should always look at the bridge of the nose' or ' look at them 80 per cent of the time'. We all know that we should 'do eye contact'; some people get very worried that they do not 'do eye contact' right. We have all heard that people when lying do not make eye contact (of course liars have heard this too so they often make very deliberate eye contact).

In fact there are no hard and fast rules about eye contact: what is appropriate for one person is threatening for another. It varies according to culture, gender, status, social experience, etc. It is important not to assume that just because someone is not making eye contact with us it means they are not listening.

> Dixon was brought up in Nigeria where it was thought rude to make eye contact with anyone older than you. When he came to England as a young man he found it very difficult to make eye contact even though he quickly picked up that he was expected to.

We get clues that the eye contact we are making with someone is right or wrong for them from their behaviour. For instance, if they feel that we are not making enough eye contact they will do all the things that people do when they feel they are not being listened to plus they just won't talk. When we overdo eye contact, people often feel threatened or uncomfortable so they might wriggle, look away, or move backwards in their seat. The important thing to remember here is that your behaviour may not be understood in the way you intended, but if you pick up the signals quickly you can correct any misunderstandings.

It is easy to get too obsessed with eye contact and if you start thinking about it during an interview you will become very self-conscious. Some recent research with children has shown that contrary to what we expect, when they are concentrating very hard on what someone is saying to them they look away (NUT 2004). Eye contact is a very important step, but it is only one of the many steps in the dance that is an active listening interaction.

Body language

All these factors are part of body language, but this term is often used specifically to refer to the way in which we use our bodies. Again there are no hard and fast rules; the way in which we use our bodies is a reflection of our personalities, but here are some actions that give clear messages. Usually we look as if we are listening when our body language is 'open', that is we do not look as if we are trying to hide ourselves or look smaller (e.g. arms wrapped around ourselves or heads down) or attacking (waving our arms around, stabbing the air, etc.). Open body language just says 'here I am, I have nothing to hide … I am listening'. See Chapter 4 for further discussion of this in relation to assertive behaviour.

Matching, mirroring

Often, when we are in rapport with someone, we unconsciously match or mirror their body language. It is quite hard to do this consciously, although you might well become aware that the person you are listening to is mirroring your behaviour, for example, sitting in the same position to you, which would tell you that they are in empathy with you. It is, however, useful to be aware of matching and mirroring when someone is demonstrating behaviour that is a long way from the behaviour you think is helpful in the situation. For instance, if someone is very agitated, or conversely, very flat or low in their mood, you do not match their behaviour because it is unlikely to be helpful if you also get very agitated or very flat.

Nods, hmms, etc.

These help things to keep moving along, but yet again it is only part of the subtle dance of communication. It is quite possible to keep saying 'mmm' when you are not listening at all, but you will not fool anyone for long.

Proximity and personal space

The way in which we position ourselves is important for making people feel comfortable and able to talk to us. Usually we get clues when people are not comfortable rather than when they are. For instance, some people need a lot of personal space and will wriggle backwards or turn away if they feel you are too close.

Our perception of comfortable personal space (the buffer zone around our body within which we feel people are too close) may be very different to those of our clients. McGuire and Priestley (1985) quote research by Kinzel, who compared the buffer zones of a group of offenders who had no history of violence with those who had a history of violence. He found that the latter had a buffer zone that was on average 3.8 times the area found comfortable by the non-violent group.

The way in which you position yourself in relation to the other person will also have an effect on listening. Face-on often feels threatening and uncomfortable, although sometimes with a desk in-between this is not the case. The ideal is probably at about half-way between 90 degrees and face-on; this gives both parties lots of opportunities to adjust their position slightly according to what feels comfortable at that moment.

An exception to this is in cars. Sitting side-by-side in cars seems to break all the rules of listening yet many people report that people really talk freely on car journeys. So, if you really want to get to know your client, you could take them on a car journey (appropriately risk-assessed beforehand, of course!).

Tone of voice
Tone of voice gives many clues about the message being transmitted. Sometimes you might have to make a conscious effort to control the tone of your voice in order to not give something away, for example, if you are trying to calm an aggressive client and are feeling frightened. On the other hand the tone of your client's voice may give you a clue to how they are feeling.

Silence
Silence is often a crucial part of active listening. Some people take a long time to gather their thoughts together and articulate them and it is important to give them time to do this. Some people who are speedy thinkers themselves, or whose style is to articulate thoughts almost as they have them, find it very difficult to wait for someone else to get around to saying something. But part of being a good listener is realising that not everyone is the same and taking account of that. If you are not sure whether the person you are trying to listen to is ever going to get round to saying something, a vague question like 'what else?' or very brief review 'so you were saying …?' may well prompt a response.

Listening reflectively
Listening does not just involve keeping quiet and hearing what someone has to say. The crucial part of reflective listening is the way you respond to what the client says. You may not be sure what they are trying to say but by reflecting you let the client know that you are interested and

are trying to work it out. (They may not be clear themselves about what they are trying to say in which case you are exploring alongside them.) Reflective listening should be posed as a statement not a question: a question requires a response and is more likely to evoke resistance.

- **Words**: It is often helpful to reflect back to people the words they actually use; this lets them know that you are in tune with them and encourages them to develop what they are trying to say. Ensure that you reflect what people really say rather than reinterpret what you think they have said. For example:
  Client: *Joe really winds me up.*
  Worker: *You say Joe winds you up,* not *do you mean that his swearing winds you up or is it his appearance?*

- **Feelings**: It is important to reflect back feelings as well as words but always be tentative.
  For example:
  Client: *Joe really winds me up.*
  Worker: *You seem quite upset about your relationship with Joe,* not *you are obviously really annoyed by Joe.*
  (Reflective listening is discussed in more detail in Chapter 5.)

Thomas Gordon (quoted in Miller and Rollnick 2002: 68) described 12 kinds of responses that are not listening and he called these roadblocks because they tend to get in the way. The underlying message of a roadblock is 'I know best'. Roadblocks include:

1 Ordering, directing, or commanding.
2 Warning, cautioning or threatening.
3 Giving advice, making suggestions, or providing solutions.
4 Persuading with logic, arguing or lecturing.
5 Telling people what they should be doing, or moralising.
6 Disagreeing, judging, criticising or blaming.
7 Agreeing, approving or praising.
8 Shaming or ridiculing.
9 Interpreting or analysing.
10 Reassuring, sympathising or consoling.
11 Questioning or probing.
12 Withdrawing, distracting, humouring or changing the subject.

There is a time and a place for most of these when they are not roadblocks (for instance in pro-social environment we often want to praise something someone has done or said); however, we do need to be aware of the danger of not listening properly to what the client is trying to say.

Using questions and reflections

- **Open questions:** In order to get people to tell you the story in some detail it is often helpful to start with open questions. Open questions are those that have a broad answer such as *'Tell me about ...'* *'How did you feel?'* *'What happened then ...?'* *Why did you do it?'* These all encourage others to elaborate on their own experience.

- **Closed questions:** Questions with a yes or no, or factual answer can be risky if overused because they limit or steer the conversation. However, they can help people focus and constructively limit what they say, or can be used to confirm factual information. For instance 'Was it Wednesday or Thursday?'

It is relatively easy to elicit lots of information by asking questions but it is also easy to evoke resistance, so wherever possible follow an open question with a reflection.

> Case manager: *How did it go when you went to see the drugs agency?*
> Client: *Well, I can't say it was the way I would have chosen to spend my day. I came out with my head buzzing.*
> Case manager: *Did you feel it was useful though?*
> Client: *I don't know ... I'm not sure ... I don't think so.*
> Pushes the client in the direction of resistance.

> Or

> Case manager: *How did it go when you went to see the drugs agency?*
> Client: *Well, I can't say it was the way I would have chosen to spend my day. I came out with my head buzzing.*
> Case manager: *Sounds like a challenging day, maybe that is inevitable at this stage.*
> Client: *I am not sure ... Yes, I suppose it is.*

The case manager's reply provokes a more reflective, less resistant response from the client.

Incremental summaries: It is often useful to stop every so often and summarise what you think you have heard. *'Can I just check I have got it straight so far ...?'* It also gives you time to make notes. It is difficult to make notes and listen at the same time unless you are gathering simple information such as name or date of birth.

What stops us listening?

Distractions and not giving people your undivided attention

It is often very hard in a busy life to give someone our undivided attention, and indeed, sometimes you will be doing things alongside clients and talking to them at the same time. It is hard to listen properly and do anything else, so ideally you should be seeking to talk to people in a quiet private setting. However, where communications might take place alongside the performance of a task you have to listen even harder to make sure you are getting the story right.

It is also important wherever possible to free yourself to give attention, so, for instance, if you are undertaking a key work session you need to take the phone off the hook and turn so that you do not keep seeing new emails popping up. Also if possible give yourself a chance to settle down, and put other distractions out of your mind; in an ideal world you would not rush straight into an important meeting or interview without a few minutes to mentally prepare.

Prejudices and stereotypes

We view the world through filters according to our prejudices and stereotypes so that if we are not careful we hear what we expect to hear rather than what is really said. Prejudices and stereotypes are triggered by all sorts of things: it may be some perception about the group of people that the client belongs to: 'Oh no, not another x, they are all the same, they don't do y', or it may be something as simple as the fact that they remind us of someone and that leads us to a particular response. We all have prejudices and stereotypes, we are kidding ourselves if we think that we do not; we make sense of the complicated nature of the social world by sorting people into groups. However, in order to listen and be truly responsive to all the individuals that we meet, we need to be aware of and challenge our own stereotypes (Chapter 7 looks at this topic in more detail).

Adaptive listening

If we do not listen to the whole story we adapt it according to what we think we are going to hear. We hear the beginning of the story and then we think 'ah, I know what they are going to say' so we fill in the ending. This is often the cause of people coming back time and time again to tell you the same story; you may never have heard what they were trying to tell you in the first place, or you may not have convinced them that you heard the story properly.

Being optimistic and solution-focused

Trotter (2004: 25) describes pro-social modelling as strengths-based – that is, it works from the position that everyone has the potential to change, even if in reality this might be a very small change. Pro-social work rewards people for the things that they do right or well, and for trying to do things better (this is discussed in Chapter 3). However difficult the client group is that we work with, if we cannot hang onto the belief that they can change, or at least some of them can change, it is probably time to look for another job.

Clients have often been judged formally or informally by society and often have been sanctioned for being deviant. They may have been in a cycle of activities that emphasise punishment and/or control for years and may have seen any short-term changes come to nothing. Our clients probably feel even more stuck and hopeless than we might on their behalf. As workers we need to convey to them our belief in their capacity to change.

So how do you convey optimism when working with difficult and challenging clients? One of the things that helps is to be aware of the evidence, to be aware of the theoretical base of what we do, and to work in a reflective way based on the best knowledge about strategies that work with our client group. Knowing that there is evidence that what we are doing and the way in which we are doing it will work with some clients allows us to approach our work with confidence and optimism. Working pro-socially comes into this category. As discussed in Chapter 1, there is an increasing body of evidence that shows that working pro-socially is effective in its positive impact on offenders. Another way to convey optimism is to work in a solution-focused way.

Working in a solution-focused way

Solution-Focused Brief Therapy is a therapy in its own right and practitioners need to be properly trained in order to practise it; however, we can borrow a few concepts and techniques which can be useful when forming empathetic and positive relationships. It is more than a set of therapeutic techniques; it is a way of thinking about the client. It is very much strengths-based. It appears deceptively simple and is attractive because it is client-centred and focused on abilities and strengths rather than assumed deficits and weaknesses. Solution-focused work is described in far more detail in O'Connell (1998).

Solution-focused work emphasises that people *have* problems rather than *are* problems and it recognises that problems happen to people in the social environment in which they operate. Solution-focused work sees people as temporarily unable to find a way around a problem (and this may include a problem with the way in which they function in society). Also it seeks out the resources that people already have and builds on those to help them to function even better.

Pro-social practice works from a clear value base about socially appropriate behaviours and attitudes, and in some cases it may be stretching credulity to suggest that clients are temporarily unable to find a way around the problems of behaving anti-socially as they may have been doing it repeatedly and for a very long time. However, nobody has all bad behaviours and taking a solution-focused perspective reminds us to value the skills and resources clients already have, even if they need to adapt those for living more pro-socially. It also reminds us to always look for the possibilities of change.

For example, anyone who has been in prison and has come out reasonably mentally intact (which is most people) will have learned a range of survival skills. These might include dealing with aggression and violence, dealing with boredom and loneliness, finding different ways to relate to different people, e.g. fellow prisoners and prison officers. These skills might need refining in order to help them survive outside prison but the foundations are there.

Optimistic and solution-focused language

In the subtleties of language we can often convey an optimistic message. Compare these two examples:

Client: *I have so many problems I feel completely overwhelmed.*
Worker: *I can see it is really difficult for you at the moment; shall we try and deal with one thing at a time? What is your biggest problem?*

Or (more solution-focused):

Client: *I have so many problems I feel completely overwhelmed.*
Worker: *I can see it is really difficult for you at the moment; what I often find most helpful is to break it down and deal with one thing at a time. Often if you can deal with one or two things some of the others fall into place. What would you like us to work on sorting out first?*

In the latter case the worker has said essentially the same thing but by using terms such as 'what I find most helpful' and 'what would you like us to work on sorting out?' (not 'what is your biggest problem?') the worker is conveying the idea that the problems can be tackled and can be solved.

It is important, however, not to overdo it. The reality is often that clients' lives are very difficult and change is very challenging, and being overly optimistic and unrealistic is going to sound to the client is if the worker is minimising their problems and is out of touch with reality.

Imagine if the worker had said: 'Oh, I am sure it is not as bad as you think, let's get started and see what we can get sorted out this morning.'

This could be described as a roadblock; it conveys the message 'I know better than you do what reality is' rather than conveying the message 'I am in touch with what is real for you but I am hopeful that we can try and work together to do something about it' (see earlier discussion of roadblocks).

Solution-focused language is always concentrated on the solution rather than the problem. (Solution-focused work also supports motivational techniques, see Chapter 5.)

For example:

Client: *I really need some help with my drinking problem.*
Worker: *Tell me about your problem, how much do you drink each day?*

Or (more solution-focused):

Client: *I really need some help with my drinking problem.*
Worker: *What would you like to change? How will you know that things are improving?*

The latter question encourages the client that change is possible and looks at where they will be after that change rather than encouraging them to focus on their problems.

Solution-focused work concentrates on:

- How the client will know that change has taken place.
- What the client wants to change.
- What the central issue is that the client wants to change rather than on the underlying cause of the problems.
- Times and places where the problems did not occur in order to build on these exceptions: in other words if you can do it/not do it once, you can do it/not do it again.
- How we can use the skills and qualities of the client.
- How the client and the worker can collaborate in the change process.
- Whether we have done enough to be satisfied.
  (Adapted from O'Connell 1998)

Solution-focused techniques

The miracle question
The miracle question is a key intervention usually used by solution-focused therapists in the first session. It concentrates on finding out what the client would like to be right, not what the client thinks is wrong. O'Connell (1998: 60) describes the question devised by Steve de Shazer as following a standard formula:

> *Imagine when you go to sleep one night a miracle occurs and the problems we have been talking about disappear. As you were asleep you did not know a miracle had happened. When you woke up what would be the first signs for you that a miracle had happened?*

It may be that the language used here is not appropriate for all client groups; not least the concept of a miracle may not work for some. However, it can be adapted:

> *If someone waved a magic wand and made everything all right what would it feel like?*

or

> *If everything were to work out for you where would you like to be in five years' time?*

For some clients talking like this might seem very extreme and unrealistic. However, O'Connell suggests that the miracle question should be preceded with something like: '*I know this might sound like a strange question but people often find it very helpful*', which acknowledges the fact that the question might seem very unrealistic but also plants the solution-focused idea that it might be useful.

Exceptions
Another useful technique borrowed from solution-focused therapy is concentrating on exceptions to the norm. This recognises that often clients have had a brief exposure to solutions but did not recognise them or acknowledge them. In this case the worker asks the client about times when the problem did not exist (however briefly), and helps them to gather information from this experience that they can use to find further solutions to the problem.

> Jake was an alcoholic. His drinking had got heavier and heavier and he had received a warning from his manager after being drunk at ⮞

work. He had been referred to an occupational counsellor. In the course of conversation he expressed his embarrassment and said that previously he had always controlled his drinking during the day so that he was sober (or at least not noticeably drunk) at work. Instead of getting bogged down in a discussion about what went wrong this time and why he was drunk at work, the counsellor encouraged him to explore all the ways in which he had controlled his daytime drinking in the past. In later sessions the counsellor encouraged Jake to build on his success in controlling his drinking in the day to controlling it more generally.

Scaling

A third useful technique from solution-focused therapy is scaling. Scaling is a useful way of getting a sense of how seriously the client views the problem, for setting goals and for monitoring progress. The response of the worker to scaling shifts it from problem focus to solution focus.

Sarah was struggling to get her teenage daughter Kirsty to go to school. This was part of a wider problem in the relationship between mother and daughter, which was reflected in Kirsty's overall behaviour. In individual interviews with the family social worker they both expressed their affection for each other and their frustration about not being able to communicate.

Worker: *On a scale of 0 to 10, where 0 is awful and 10 is brilliant where would you say your relationship with Kirsty is at the moment?*
Sarah: *About 2.*
Worker: *What stops it becoming a 1?*

By this response the worker has moved Sarah away from thinking about what is wrong in her relationship with Kirsty to what is right and the worker will then help her to build on it. The perception of where she is on the scale is purely subjective for Sarah; the worker does not need an explanation. Another response might have been: 'How do you think you could get it to 2½?'

In my experience clients catch on very quickly to the concept of scaling and find it useful shorthand for reporting progress.

Summary

In order to influence people we need to form empathetic relationships with them.

Empathy on its own is not enough because empathy alone can be interpreted as collusion; it needs to be supported by clear pro-social values demonstrated by reinforcement of pro-social actions and expressions and discouragement of anti-social actions and expressions.

When interacting with others the meaning of the communication is in the way the receiver interprets it which is not necessarily what we meant to say, so we need to constantly check that we have understood what they meant to tell us and they have understood what we are trying to tell them. We do this by active and reflective listening.

Skills for active and reflective listening include:

- appropriate eye contact
- appropriate body language
- matching and mirroring
- nods, hmms, etc.
- sensitivity to proximity and personal space
- taking account of tone of voice
- silence
- listening reflectively
- using questions and reflections
- incremental summaries.

Things that stop us listening include:

- distractions and not giving people our undivided attention
- prejudices and stereotypes
- adaptive listening.

Communication is like a dance where each partner is constantly making minute adjustments to stay in harmony with their partner, and just like a dance, in communications everyone is different.

Pro-social practice is optimistic and solution-focused.

Solution-focused work is not simply a set of techniques; it is another way of looking at the same world.

Solution-Focused Brief Therapy is a therapy in its own right but we can borrow some techniques from it. Useful techniques are:

- using optimistic and solution-focused language
- the miracle question
- exceptions
- scaling.

3. Exploring the legitimate use of authority: roles, rules, values, expectations and rewards

'I wouldn't have minded getting detention so much because I knew I was breaking the rules about uniform, but I only wore my Doc Martens because Kate has been wearing hers for weeks. She didn't get detention. I feel like they were picking on me and it's not fair.'

Introduction

Underpinning pro-social practice is the legitimate use of the authority vested in the practitioner by their role. This means being clear about what the rules are and applying them consistently and fairly. In order to do this practitioners need to be open and transparent with themselves and their clients about the values underpinning their work and how these manifest themselves in their practice.

Like many tenets of pro-social modelling this seems like common sense but is much harder to do in practice than in theory. Also like many things in pro-social work this is not a technique, but a way of thinking which permeates all aspects of practice.

The legitimate use of authority is referred to throughout this book. This chapter defines it, and also discusses values and the links to practice, in order to help the practitioner work in an ethical way, balancing respect for the client with organisational and social expectations.

The legitimate use of authority

Much of the research into pro-social modelling (e.g. Bottoms 2004; Rex and Maltravers 1999; McIvor 1998) has demonstrated how important the legitimate use of authority is to pro-social practice. In describing a pilot project using pro-social modelling to underpin Community Service (now called Community Punishment), Rex (2004: 76) says:

The way in which they used their authority was seen as one way in which probation officers exemplified what kinds of behaviour they were seeking to encourage in the people they supervised. As such, it was seen as to enhance the 'modelling' aspect of pro-social modelling, and as helping to explain why practitioners using this type of approach might hope to exert a positive influence on offenders.

Take, for instance, the ongoing debate about racism in the police force. If an individual police officer or a police force is considered racist then they will still be able to operate as law enforcers but very few people (and particularly people from minority ethnic groups) are going to see them as positive role models. They are not going to say, 'I would like to be like that; I can see they are really trying hard to do the decent thing to help this community; I think I might become a police officer.'

Sadly, illegitimate use of authority and negative role modelling are often far more powerful and far more enduring than legitimate use of authority. The police are finding to their cost that their many and strenuous efforts to overcome racism in the force are attracting far less attention than the negative message about ongoing racism.

Bottoms *et al.* (2001: 90) describes the four main kinds of compliant (obedient) behaviour:

1   **Instrumental/prudential compliance** based on self-interested calculation. Principal mechanisms include incentives and disincentives.
2   **Normative compliance** based on a felt moral obligation, commitment or attachment. Principal mechanisms include acceptance of or belief in the norm; attachment leading to compliance (e.g. a changing perspective due to gaining a new partner or becoming a parent) and legitimacy.
3   **Constraint-based compliance** derived from some kind of constraint or coercion. Principal mechanisms include physical restrictions (natural or imposed), restrictions on access to the target (e.g. better security of cars) or structural constraints.
4   **Compliance based on habit or routine**.

Many of the mechanisms to secure compliance may be present in the client–worker relationship – for instance, in criminal justice, constraint-based compliance is always present to a greater or lesser degree. However, the evidence (fairly slight but consistent according to Bottoms and Rex (1998: 21)) suggests that when authority is seen as being exercised legitimately, that is the person in authority is behaving in the way that the subject considers it is morally right and proper for them to do in their role, normative compliance is engendered and lasting change is more likely.

McIvor (1998) found in her study of Community Punishment in Scotland that a 'firm but fair' approach by supervisors increased compliance. This included responding consistently to non-compliance and also rewarding compliance.

Rex (2004) discusses the emerging indications that Community Punishment may reduce recidivism when compared with a short prison service for similar offences. The (limited) research in this area indicates that people see a sentence of Community Punishment as fair and they also undergo constructive experiences in undertaking work that helps the community. Reductions in reoffending also come about when the offender sees the sentence as a consequence of their own behaviour, not the judge's (Rex 2004: 78). This suggests that sentencers need to make efforts to explain sentences so that recipients see them as fair. The same principle would apply in other settings: for instance, in a social work setting clients need to understand the consequences of their actions, and if these consequences come about, to believe that this is fair.

Bottoms *et al.* (2001: 104) refer to the Milwaukee Domestic Violence Experiment that demonstrated that the fairness or otherwise of the conduct of arresting officers seems to have long-term consequences for the subsequent compliance of arrestees with the law prohibiting domestic violence.

The Woolf Report (1991) into the Strangeways prison riot in 1990 concluded that the riots were a protest against the way in which the prisoners were being treated. Woolf recommended an improvement in what he called justice; this included a fair and transparent system of adjudication where this materially affected the prisoner.

As Player and Jenkins say (1993: 9):

> Stability in prisons rests on there being a proper balance between three elements of the prison regimes: security arrangements to prevent prisoners escaping; control measures to prevent disruption and disorder within establishments, and procedures for justice to ensure all prisoners are dealt with humanity and fairness.

Prisons can only run with the cooperation of the prisoners; there are not enough staff to ensure constraint-based compliance in most cases. Prisoners are much more likely to be compliant if they believe that the rules and the way in which they are enforced are legitimate.

Whitemoor Prison has recently changed the regime in its segregation unit from very strict control (with very little interpersonal contact between prisoners and prison officers) to a regime that the unit manager calls a 'therapeutic alliance type environment' (Fenwick 2005: 10). This transformation has resulted in a large reduction in the number of times extreme force (mechanical restraints or the use of physical force) has been used.

The components of legitimacy (adapted from Rex and Maltravers (1998: 21) and Bottoms *et al.* (2001: 77)) are:

1   **Representation**: Has the client had the opportunity to play a part in the making of important decisions, have they had an opportunity to tell their side of the story and be listened to?
2   **Consistency**: Are clients treated the same as others and the same over a period of time? Clients can pick this up by seeing the way that others are treated as well as themselves.
3   **Impartiality**: Does the client believe that they have not been treated unfairly because of the worker's personal bias? For instance, that they have not been treated differently due to their race, gender, or sexuality.
4   **Accuracy**: Does the worker demonstrate an ability to make important decisions based on an ability to use valid, reliable data and being open about the process?
5   **Correctability**: Can decisions be corrected if proved to be wrong is there a right of appeal, for instance?
6   **Ethicality**: Are clients treated with respect and dignity, demonstrating that they are valued members of society?

The influence of values on practice

None of us works in a value-free environment. Even practice described as 'client-centred' is underpinned by the worker's value that the client should set the agenda. Pro-social modelling is underpinned by a clear set of values that both value the individual and recognise the importance of encouraging that individual to conform to wider social expectations. Carl Rogers (1951), a leading proponent of client-centred work, proposed that people are more likely to take responsibility for change in a climate of well-directed empathy, warmth and genuineness. Rogerian therapists encourage the client to set the agenda and see the therapist as facilitators of the client's journey towards their goals; they do not see it as their role to steer the client in any particular direction.

As described in Chapter 2 research has shown (Trotter 1999) that when working with offenders, empathy alone can be seen as collusive and can encourage the client to continue anti-social behaviour. Also that change is most likely to happen when it is undertaken with clear encouragement of pro-social behaviours and expressions and clear discouragement of anti-social behaviours and expressions.

41

Whose values are the principal influence?

By definition, the unwilling or difficult client is unlikely to be self-directed towards positive change, at least in the first instance, although many may want to change but feel unable to do something about it. Also these clients are subject to interventions because someone else has decided that they need to change. For instance, a court, a juvenile panel, a teacher, or a social worker has decided that they need to stop offending, or being a nuisance in the community or at school, or drinking or taking drugs or they need to look after their children better.

Additionally the worker is likely to be judged by their ability to bring about change in their clients, particularly when, taking the criminal justice system as an example, this is the explicit aim of the organisation. The prison service and the probation service (currently being combined at a strategic level into the National Offender Management Service) and the Youth Justice Board all have the objective of reducing reoffending. The rehabilitation of offenders (helping them to change towards more pro-social behaviour) is not the only way that these services are expected to do this.

The probation service has five aims:

1   Protecting the public.
2   Reducing reoffending.
3   The proper punishment of offenders in the community.
4   Ensuring offenders' awareness of the effects of crime on the victims of crime and the public.
5   Rehabilitation of offenders.

Only in the last two aims does the offender, and the possibility for the offender to change, move to the fore.

The prison service has a statement of purpose (2004):

> 'Her Majesty's Prison Service serves the public by keeping in custody those committed by the courts. Our duty is to look after them with humanity and help them lead law-abiding and useful lives in custody and after release.'

Of course the prison service's primary purpose is to keep people safely locked up when the courts have designated that they should do so. Prisons usually have a small number of staff to look after a large number of people. The reality is that a great deal of time and energy is taken up in the day-to-day demands of housing large numbers of people, keeping them fed and under control and moving them around the prison.

The prison service has made great steps towards being a more humane organisation in the last few years with policies on (and a genuine commitment to) safe custody and anti-discriminatory practice. Many prison officers see their job as far more than just managing large groups of people. However, the reality is that prison officers are more likely to be judged negatively if there is a riot, or someone commits suicide or escapes, than be judged positively on the more intangible matters of whether they treat people with humanity or increase the chances of them becoming law-abiding citizens when released.

Managing the tension between building an empathetic relationship and implementing the rules

Pro-social work underpins all the aims above. Treating people humanely, helping them to grow and change as people, is integral to reducing offending, to reducing the risks of disorder in prisons and in other institutions such as schools and hostels, and to improving people's ability to live with others. But how does the worker manage this tension? On the one hand the worker is trying to build up an empathetic relationship which will allow them to steer and influence the client towards pro-social behaviour and away from anti-social behaviour. On the other hand there is always the risk that if the client breaks the rules of the system of which the worker is a part, even if the rule-breaking is not connected to the relationship with the worker, sanctions will come into play that may end or severely damage that relationship.

A social worker working with a family to keep the children at home has to make clear to the parents that the safety and interests of the children are paramount and if at any time they believe the children to be at increased risk they will have to remove them from the family. However, they also need to try and build a relationship so that if problems arise and they have to exercise their authority in this way, they can still continue to work with the family.

The only answer to managing the tension between being client-focused yet working within strict boundaries is to be very clear with yourself and the client about your role and the rules and boundaries. For many workers balancing the dual roles of helper and agent of social control can feel uncomfortable, but working in a pro-social way balances these two roles because it encourages clarity about what is desired behaviour and the consequences of undesired behaviour.

Role clarification and boundaries

Trotter (1999, 2004) refers to several research studies that indicate that the outcomes for the client were much better if the worker and the client had frequently discussed and clarified why they were there, what they were doing and what the boundaries of the relationship were. Jones and Alcabes (cited in Trotter 1999) described this as the process of client socialisation, where the client needs to accept their role and what is expected of them, and understand and accept how the worker can help before any progress can be made.

Clarification of role starts at the very beginning of work with the client and includes clarifying the role of the agency as a whole as well as the individuals with in it. At the beginning of a Community Order (formerly a Community Rehabilitation Order or Probation Order) offenders will be told by their supervising officer what the order is about, what is expected of the client and what he or she can expect from the supervising officer and others that they might come into contact with. This process might be repeated if, for instance, the offender takes part in an accredited programme (structured group work) where one of the first activities will be to establish ground rules that say 'this is how we are going to work together'. Similarly, on entry to prison the prisoner will be told the prison rules and also about how he or she can expect to be treated.

In a less structured setting there is still a need to establish who is client and who is worker. For instance, a new entrant to a youth club might be greeted by a worker and introduced to other staff; the worker might show them around or tell them the ground rules, thus establishing that the worker is not just one of the gang but, however friendly, has a separate and distinct role. This kind of action will put the worker in a much better position to take a more directive role if necessary, such as enforcing a rule or thanking (rewarding) someone for a pro-social action such as helping without being asked.

Pro-social modelling is very much a team activity (see organisational modelling in Chapter 1) and it is essential that all staff are singing from the same song sheet when clarifying and reinforcing the role boundaries. It is important where agencies are using volunteers – and other workers who may not be familiar with working with these client groups – that the staff are trained to understand the nature of their role and how to conduct themselves accordingly.

Hostels often have several staff such as cooks, cleaners and maintenance staff, who may have quite a lot of interactions with clients. These staff may meet clients in a more informal and relaxed setting and can be powerful pro-social role models and influences, but they need to be confident in their role and aware of its boundaries and be able to assert this to the client if necessary. In other words both worker and client need to know that they are worker and client and while they can have **friendly relationships**, they are not **friends** with all the connotations of reciprocity and equality that that implies. If the roles are not clear to client, worker, or both, there is a real danger that the worker can be drawn into risky relationships with the client and possibly to colluding with anti-social behaviour.

Sometimes the boundary between empathising with the client and colluding with them is a very fine line.

> Steve worked in an agency supporting illegal drug users. He cared deeply about his work and his clients and over a period of time he started using the street language of drug users. This undoubtedly helped him to get close to his clients but it also made it difficult for the clients to see him as anything other than one of them. His unquestioning use of their language and concepts to describe drug use, drug paraphernalia, getting drugs and the drugs themselves – even when they knew he did not use drugs himself – implied that he thought this was at best normal and at worst romantic or exciting.
>
> During supervision Steve had to be helped to take a step back, to make it clear to his clients that while he respected them and cared for them, he did not think it was OK to live in the world of a drug abuser and he was trying to help them to move out of that world.

During ongoing relationships between the client and the worker roles and rules need to be clarified regularly. Aspects of the role that need to be clarified might include (adapted from Trotter 2004, Ch 3):

- Who is the primary client? For instance, in a child protection case the primary client is the child and their needs will be paramount.
- What the worker can and cannot do.
- What the worker will and will not talk about, for instance, the level of personal disclosure by the worker that it is acceptable to expect. Trotter (2004) quotes Schulman, who suggests that if a client asks a personal question such as 'do you have children?', the worker should think about the meaning behind the question (in this case the client might be exploring whether the worker has the capacity to understand) and reply accordingly.
- What information will be passed on, and to whom.
- The boundaries of acceptable behaviour and attitudes.

Trotter's research (2004) into child protection workers demonstrates that the best client outcomes were associated with workers who regularly and frequently clarified their role, but he also found that very few workers did this.

What are the rules, what is negotiable?

It is very important when working pro-socially to ensure that the client does actually know what the rules are and what is and is not negotiable. Often rules and expectations are introduced at the beginning of the client–worker relationship, if at all, and then not reiterated until there is a problem. In order to work legitimately the rules and expectations have to be transparent to the client.

One factor to consider is how does the client gain access to the rules? If, for instance, they are written down can the client read them? A recent analysis (Lewis and Davies 2004) of the standard rules for Probation Service Approved Premises (hostels) showed them to have a readability level of 16: in other words, they could only be read with ease by a resident with a reading level sufficient to gain GCSEs A*–C. Approximately 1 in 10 of offenders have reading skills at this level, so 9 out of 10 residents probably cannot read and understand the rules.

In order to maintain legitimacy, clients and workers also need to be clear about rules and expectations that apply to the worker and a good example of this is confidentiality. Confidentiality is often misunderstood. The boundaries of confidentiality need to be made clear from the outset and reinforced at regular intervals. Clients may not be happy that nothing they say to their worker is truly confidential – as is probably the case in many criminal justice settings or in child protection, for instance – but they are far more likely to be unhappy in the long run if they find that something has been passed on that they thought they were saying in confidence.

Values underpinning pro-social practice

In 1998 Her Majesty's Inspectorate of Probation produced the following statement of values (Chapman and Hough 1998: 18) that underpin effective practice with offenders. These are:

- An uncompromising stance against the harm caused by crime.
- A strong belief in the capacity of people to change.
- The importance of taking personal responsibility for change.
- The necessity of learning from partnership.
- The values of partnership.
- Social inclusion.
- Public accountability.

With a few adjustments to the words (replace the word 'crime' with others such as 'anti-social behaviour' or 'drug use') I think this is a useful statement of values that underpin much pro-social work. The values of an organisation will be symbolised by the rules, rewards and sanctions that the organisation or individual workers put in place.

In a sense these are formal values, or overarching values. Everyday practice, and particularly the things that we choose to encourage, are based on what we as an individual or team think are important. Some of this will not be written down but will reflect our informal values. This is discussed in the next section of this chapter. Values, particularly in the context of diversity, are also discussed in Chapter 9.

Rewards, sanctions and values

In order to change behaviour you need to change the rewards and costs associated with that behaviour (Bonta 2002). Punishment (sanctions), even when it leads to short-term behaviour change, can also lead to a self-fulfilling prophesy where the subject comes to believe they are 'bad' because they are being punished, and therefore 'acts bad' (Huesmann and Podolski 2004: 66).

Taking an overview of research over the last 30 years, Huesmann and Podolski say a very important influence on behaviour is observational learning. Indeed this is the basis of the 'modelling' part of pro-social modelling. Applied to punishment this suggests that seeing punishment done to oneself or others is likely to increase the chances of the subject meting out similar behaviour. In summary, punishment models aggression and can lead to aggression.

It can be argued that anyone under the supervision of the Offender Management Services and their partners is receiving (and has received) a considerable amount of punishment. Other clients who are not subject to formal sanctions may not feel that they are actively being punished but they may feel ambiguous about the client–worker relationship. On the one hand they may appreciate the time and attention, on the other they may resent the infringement on their time and freedom even if it is only because they have to make themselves available for visits or meetings. It is unlikely that they will feel that the relationship is intrinsically rewarding.

Punishment only suppresses behaviour; it does not extinguish it (Huesmann and Podolski 2004). Extinction of behaviour often comes when the effect of undesirable behaviour (to the subject) is neutral, that is no punishment or reward, and desirable behaviour is rewarded. Obviously there are limits to how far you can take this in a working environment and clients often need to be told when their behaviour is undesirable (not pro-social). However, in everyday interactions it is often possible to ignore low-level 'bad' behaviour and encourage better behaviour by acknowledging and rewarding it.

Pro-social modelling is a positive, reward-driven model and staff are encouraged to look out for every opportunity to reward the behaviours that they want to encourage. However, we have to be realistic and recognise that there will be a number of rules and sanctions in most settings which are not negotiable. Rewards often drive behaviour change, but have to be delivered in the context of existing rules and laws.

My experience of working with staff, particularly in a residential setting, is that it's easy to slip into a sanction-driven environment. Where there are rules and sanctions in place, if we are going to encourage behaviour change, we have to work to generate rewards and encourage positive behaviour: in other words to develop a reward-driven environment. We also have to take into account that many clients (and staff) will be unused to hearing anything positive about themselves and therefore we have to make sure that they have heard and believed us when we say positive things.

Dean was imprisoned on the juvenile wing of a Young Offender Institution (prison). He was young and frightened and he wanted and needed lots of adult attention. He got this by creating a series of crises where he had accidents, felt suddenly ill or precipitated some kind of incident. The staff were getting crosser and crosser with him, they did not have time to give him so much attention and he was becoming extremely irritating. Even though Dean was getting negative attention, it was adult attention so his behaviour was being rewarded in a paradoxical way.

Fortunately, despite the fact that they were busy and did not have much time to deal with one child, the staff recognised how needy Dean was. They worked together to either ignore Dean's naughty behaviour, or where that was not possible, to deal with it with the minimum of fuss. They took the time to speak to him whenever they could when he was behaving reasonably, and whenever possible to comment positively on his behaviour. Over a period of time Dean calmed down and enjoyed the more positive relationship he had with staff, and also with fellow young prisoners who found him less irritating.

What do we want to reward?

We want to reward pro-social behaviour and expressions, anything that is bringing the client to a socially acceptable and law-abiding life. However, what does this mean in practice in everyday interactions?

I often ask participants in training events to identify what behaviour they want to encourage in their clients. The lists they come up with vary although they have many common factors. They will probably include the following (in no particular order):

- cooperating with the practitioner
- not taking things for granted
- saying thanks
- extra effort
- showing patience
- coming in not under the influence of drink or drugs
- saying hello
- consideration of others
- putting things away
- doing extra things they do not have to do
- volunteering
- personal hygiene
- trying to look presentable

- expressing pro-social/anti-crime views
- listening to instructions
- taking turns
- punctuality
- attending other agencies
- taking part in programmes/activities
- completing a task
- trying to engage
- trying to solve problems
- showing some victim empathy
- doing chores
- good behaviour
- being a positive influence

The things that people want to encourage demonstrate what they think is important and therefore their underlying values. I have already identified that all staff who interact with the client are on show and are role models, therefore it is essential that both individual workers and staff teams give a consistent message about what is important in the way they behave both towards clients and towards one another. In other words they need to ensure that they give consistent messages otherwise the pro-social message will be undermined.

It is extremely useful for a team to examine what they want to reward and discuss, and how they are going to support one another in doing this consistently (see the exercise in Appendix C).

One worker in a project found swearing really offensive whereas another viewed it as so commonplace as to be not worth getting excited about. The first worker challenged clients and asked them not to swear; the second worker ignored swearing. The more sensitive clients learned to regulate their swearing in front of one worker but did not learn that, in fact, swearing is offensive to many people, and did not learn that controlling use of offensive language is a social asset in many settings. ➲

The team had a discussion about what pro-social behaviours they wanted to encourage. They had a discussion about swearing where the two workers expressed their different points of view. This led the whole team to decide that the majority did not like swearing and although they would put up with a bit of it, an incontinent stream of 'F' and 'C' words did irritate them. They then decided to talk individually to the worst culprits about this, encourage them to try hard not to swear and to reward them for **trying** not to swear (accepting that they were going to slip up frequently).

The worker who did not think swearing was a big deal was persuaded that her view was different to her colleagues and to go along with the rest of the team. She laughingly agreed to try to swear less herself and subsequently told the clients that she too was struggling to change her behaviour. The member of staff who hated swearing continued to be very strict about it but she tried to look out for when the clients (and her colleague) were trying not to swear, and to reward them for trying.

The outcome was that clients and staff became much more self-conscious about swearing and its impact on other people and were therefore better able to control their behaviour.

What do we mean by rewards?

Most rewards are informal and often verbal. They could be described as affirmations. Concrete rewards may on some occasions be appropriate but care needs to be taken to ensure that they are legitimate and appropriate.

Rewards might include:

- praise
- thanks
- star charts
- telling others
- trip out
- whole project activity
- giving time, doing something with a member of staff
- writing praise in record, telling case manager, etc. (tell client that you have done it)

- giving responsibility
- cup of tea
- public praise
- thank you note
- giving opportunities
- acknowledging efforts
- material rewards (small/ token, e.g. bar of chocolate, etc.)
- points system (do not make it too complicated or long-term)

Having a variety of small rewards is important but often the ones that make the most impact are the simplest and easiest to give, such as saying 'thank you'. Often there is little or no scope for using material rewards and they might not be appropriate. However, the practitioner is always likely to have opportunities to give positive feedback and praise even if, in the first instance, it is only for turning up or receiving a visit.

Rex (2004) points out that clients need to be clear what they are being rewarded for; they also need to perceive the reward as a reward. For instance, a reduction in appointments with a supervisor (referring to probation), who is seen as helpful and supportive, may not be seen as a reward. Research undertaken by Bonta and Rugge (2004) in Manitoba, Canada, demonstrated that probation officers spend remarkably little time addressing criminogenic needs (factors related to offending). In this case it is unlikely that clients perceive themselves as being rewarded for, and therefore encouraged towards, anti-criminal behaviour.

Giving and hearing praise is often unfamiliar. In Chapter 4 there is a section on how to give pro-social praise.

The legitimate use of rewards

Guidance on the use of sanctions and rewards in work with young people in secure accommodation (YJB 2000) identifies the requirements to ensure that the system is seen as relevant and fair, in other words, legitimate. They need to have:

- **Transparency**: it must be clear how people can get rewards and what they are being rewarded for.
- **Consistency**: they need to be applied equally to different people in different situations (this is not always possible: for instance, in a hostel there may be people on different kinds of order or on bail, or in prisons there may be people at different stages in their sentences. Be clear about what rewards apply to what category of person).
- **Justice**: the reward needs to be seen to be in proportion to the achievement and applied fairly.
- **Equality of access**: as far as is possible (see above) everyone should have equal access to rewards.
- **Achievability**: rewards should be achievable (often you will be rewarding effort not achievement).

Margaret worked in a juvenile secure unit (local authority secure children's home). She cared deeply about the young people she key worked with and she sometimes bought CDs and posters for them when she thought they were doing particularly well. On a training event she had a chance to work with others to discuss rewards and sanctions and compare them with the systems used in other institutions. When she thought about this further it was clear that although her reward system was motivated by a kind concern for young people who did not have many treats, the system was not legitimate. The young people did not know what rewards they were going to get and what they were going to get them for; the material rewards could well be seen as disproportionately large. The other young people with whom she was not involved had no opportunity to get access to similar rewards.

Sometimes the reward in itself may cause concern – until recently some juvenile institutions used cigarettes as a reward. These were very popular and motivating rewards for the young people. However, as the young people were below the age where they would legally be able to buy cigarettes, and allowing young people access to cigarettes is against Youth Justice Board policy, by no stretch of the imagination could the rewards be described as legitimate or pro-social.

The rewards systems that worked best with young people were simple and clear about the purpose of rewards. Also they operated over a short time period so that the young people could remember what they were being rewarded for, and were based on a positive incremental system rather than a negative one. For example, if the system consisted of building up points they would not then lose those points even if they later did something wrong. This is fairer because whatever the young person did subsequently, they had, at one point, done something that justified a reward and this should not be taken from them.

Developing a more positive environment

One bonus for staff is that if you start to look for positive things you tend to find them, which gives a more optimistic feel to the work. Staff, of course, should also be looking for things to reward among themselves; the reward may well consist simply of a 'thank you' (see Chapter 4 for how to give a positive praise message using pro-social feedback).

When teams are struggling with a difficult client group they can sometimes develop a collective gloom and pessimism. One way of countering this and building mutual reward and optimism into team culture is to have a 'good news' spot in every team meeting. My experience is that at first staff may struggle to think of any good news but after a time they will start to look out for good news and they will find it. Then they need to congratulate one another on their achievements. The research into pro-social modelling in South Yorkshire (Henry *et al.* 2000) demonstrated that staff found working pro-socially motivating; it was little things like a more positive and rewarding atmosphere that made the difference.

> Staff in a Probation Approved Premise (hostel) do room checks every week. If a room was really dirty and smelly they used to put a notice on the door telling the occupant that the room must be cleaned up. As result of a discussion about how to generate a more positive environment the staff started putting a notice on everybody's doors. If the rooms were clean and tidy the notice said 'thank you for keeping your room clean and tidy'. They realised after a few weeks that several of the residents were displaying their notices on the wall of their room and the overall standard of cleanliness had gone up.

Frequently asked questions about rewards and sanctions

Why should we reward people for doing things they should be doing anyway and/or when they are offenders?
We are not talking about rewarding people for the behaviour that brought them into the project in the first place (including being offenders). We are talking about rewarding people for behaviour change or attempted behaviour change. The bottom line is that rewards work; not only are they likely to drive behaviour change, but working with a positive focus also improves the general working atmosphere.

The report into pro-social modelling in South Yorkshire hostels (Henry *et al.* 2000) describes how many staff say that consciously rewarding people had helped to make a difference to their behaviour. One member of staff said 'the residents seem to come to me for help if needed and will help me more' (p. 32).

Nobody is going to take me seriously if I keep saying 'please', 'thank you' and 'well done' all the time.
Henry *et al.* 2000 also found that offering more praise and rewards made the most difference in the hostel and the rewards that had the most impact were simple informal rewards such as saying 'please' and 'thank you'. One domestic supervisor described a situation in which s/he rewarded three residents who had helped to take laundry upstairs. Their packets of crisps were put on one side with a thank you note. When they came back they were given the crisps but still asked for the thank you note. Pro-

social feedback (Chapter 4) will help you to give a positive and sincere praise message. A good place to start giving positive rewards is within the staff team. This is a good piece of modelling if the clients see you rewarding one another.

Sanctions

When working pro-socially, sanctions should always be the last resort rather than the first; however, if they are necessary they should also be legitimate, i.e. based on a clear ethical framework understood and implemented by all staff. They should also be:

- **Transparent**: it needs to be clear what the rules are and the consequences of breaking them. This includes making sure that people have the means to find out what the rules are. Sometimes this is as simple (or complicated) as ensuring that the client can read the rules.
- **Consistent**: they need to be applied equally to different people for the same thing. Sometimes different people in the same setting are subject to different rules. In this case you need to be transparent about this even if it is not appropriate to say who is subject to which rules.
- **Just**: the sanction needs to be seen to be just, i.e. in proportion to the misdemeanour. This is one of the problems of a 'three strikes and you're out' policy as often the third misdemeanour may lead to a punishment that appears to be completely out of proportion to the offence and thus unjust.
- **Access to appeal**: there should be some system in place whereby the recipient of the sanction can appeal.

Summary

Underpinning pro-social practice is the legitimate use of the authority vested in the practitioner by their role.

A 'fair but firm' approach increases compliance.

The components of legitimacy are:

- representation
- consistency
- impartiality
- accuracy
- correctability
- ethicality.

Pro-social practice is underpinned by a clear set of values and these manifest themselves in rules, but also in the behaviours and expressions that workers encourage or discourage.

Workers need to be very clear with themselves and with clients about their role and the boundaries of their role.

Workers also need to be clear what the rules are and what is negotiable.

Punishment is unlikely to lead to long-term behaviour change.

Pro-social modelling is a positive, reward-driven model and wherever possible the emphasis needs to be on encouraging behaviour through praise and reward, rather than discouraging behaviour through sanctions.

Workers in teams need to decide what behaviour they want to encourage and how they can operate consistently.

Workers also need to reward one another. There is evidence that working in this way is motivating for staff.

Rewards and sanctions need to be legitimate: that is, they need to be seen to be transparent, to be implemented consistently, to be just, to have equality of access and to be achievable. They need to be delivered within a clear ethical framework understood and operated by all staff.

4. Assertive interactions and pro-social feedback

'I really like my social worker. She is no pushover but I think she genuinely cares about me. She has really helped me to behave differently by telling me what she likes and doesn't like about what I do and why. I found it a bit scary at first but now I realise that she is trying to help me I find it useful.'

Introduction

As discussed in the previous chapter, in order to work pro-socially practitioners need to identify what their underlying values are. They also need to understand how this translates into desirable behaviour that they want to encourage and undesirable behaviour that they want to discourage. They need to work out how they are going to encourage this desirable behaviour by rewarding or affirming it. The emphasis will be on rewarding rather than applying sanctions, but the practitioner needs to be clear where they draw the line, what behaviours they are not willing to accept, and ensure that the clients also know what the rules are and the consequences of breaking them.

Pro-social practice needs to be consistent throughout the whole organisation, so teams need to be 'singing from the same song sheet'. Team members need to agree what behaviours they are all going to encourage or discourage and how they are going to do this so that they give a consistent message and actively support one another's practice. Individuals and teams also need to be aware that they are on show and the behaviour that they model towards one another and clients will be picked up and copied by the clients.

However, none of this is going to have any effect if the clients do not know what they are being rewarded for or what they should be doing differently. Neither is it going to work if the client feels that he or she is being lectured and that the worker has made no effort to see things from their point of view.

> Jack was in a Juvenile Secure Unit; he hated it and was constantly grumpy and uncooperative. Benjamin, his key worker, was persistently friendly and patient and was beginning to get a positive response from Jack. One morning Jack started the day really well, he said good morning and helped lay the breakfast table, and then also helped to clear up. He was less grumpy and more forthcoming all morning, but at lunchtime he got into a squabble with one of the other boys and was sent to his room to calm down. After a while Benjamin went to talk to him.
>
> 'You did really well this morning, your attitude was much better, but you really disappointed me at lunchtime. I would like to see a bit more of this morning's Jack and less of lunchtime's Jack. I would like you to think about what you are going to do and I will come back and talk to you later.' He left Jack bewildered. How did it all go wrong? What had he done right this morning what should he do more of, or less of? Was it really worth trying?

Benjamin could have given Jack much more guidance about what behaviours he liked and would like to encourage. The primary motive for sending Jack to his room was to allow him time to cool off but it would still have felt like punishment to a young person, so the point that he had behaved badly had been made. Benjamin could have helped Jack far more by working out with him what he could have done to avoid the situation. He could have let Jack see that he was trying to understand his point of view, while still being clear about what he (Benjamin) thought was right and wrong.

This chapter introduces assertive pro-social feedback, which enables us to tell the client what behaviours we want to encourage and, if necessary, discourage. It helps the client to hear what we are saying and to engage in the change process because the message is clear and understandable and the interpretation of the message is negotiated with the client. Interacting assertively is a skill that can be used in many more contexts than giving pro-social feedback and this will be addressed first.

Assertiveness

Assertiveness is often misunderstood and misinterpreted. It is sometimes seen as a means of getting your own way or dominating people and is frequently regarded with some trepidation by people as a behaviour that might bring negative consequences. This stems from a misunderstanding of the concept. Assertiveness is much more than a way of behaving. More fundamentally it is a way of thinking about people, that is, valuing and respecting others while at the same time valuing and respecting yourself.

Behaving assertively can be extremely effective in working in an open and honest way with people while not losing sight of one's own beliefs and needs. It can be an effective way of preventing, reducing and managing conflict, and is a fundamental skill for working pro-socially.

Willis and Daisley (1995) suggest that assertiveness has its roots in the American Civil Rights Movement of the 1960s. It was recognised that black people needed to find a way to cope with the discrimination and aggression that they faced and fighting aggression with aggression did not seem to be effective. It was not acceptable to just submit passively to the behaviour that was meted out to them, especially as this left them feeling frustrated and angry and did not change anything. The work on assertion involved developing a series of techniques that people could use in a controlled and mindful way. Using these techniques elicited a radically different response from the oppressors and the oppressed, the former stopped, listened and in some cases changed their behaviour and the latter felt more powerful and gained self-respect because they had stood up for themselves in a positive way.

Also in the 1960s and 1970s, Thomas Harris (1970), developing ideas from Transactional Analysis, built on the work of Eric Berne (1964) which he described as being about the 'games that people play' in relationships with one another. The exciting thing about this work was the concept that we can become conscious of the patterns in our behaviour and we can change the way in which we behave.

Harris (in Willis and Daisley 1995: 3) described underlying behaviours based on four 'life positions' that were dependent on the way we feel about others and ourselves:

1 I'm not OK – you are OK, underlies passivity.
2 I'm not OK – you are not OK, underlies depression.
3 I'm OK – you are not OK, underlies aggression.
4 I'm OK – you are OK, underlies assertion.

The first three of these life positions and consequent behaviours have evolved as a result of conditioning in earlier life. Passive behaviour and aggressive behaviour are instinctive; when animals feel threatened they fight or run away (fight or flight) and the behaviour that humans instinctively show when they feel threatened is simply a version of this.

The concept of consciously deciding 'we are both OK and I am going to behave accordingly' underlies all the development and subsequent theories of assertion.

Since the 1960s assertiveness has gained increasing currency as a self-conscious way of behaving towards other people. In the 1970s and 1980s assertiveness training for women was seen as a very important way of giving women the power to survive and compete in a man's world. Over time assertiveness has increasingly been seen not as a series of techniques (although some are very useful) but as a way of thinking about people which in turn leads to a way of behaving.

Developing assertiveness skills is now considered to be valuable for anyone who has to interact with others, including practitioners, managers and clients.

A definition of assertiveness

Assertiveness is a form of behaviour that demonstrates your respect for yourself and for others. This means that assertiveness is concerned with dealing with your own feelings about yourself and other people, as much as with the end result (Willis and Daisley 1995: 12).

Assertiveness means:

- Standing up for your rights in such a way that you do not violate other people's rights.
- Expressing your needs, preferences and feelings in a manner that is neither threatening nor punishing to others and without undue fear or anxiety.
- Direct honest communication between individuals which assumes that they are able to interact equally and take responsibility for themselves (Back and Back 1991: 1).

Understanding assertiveness

Assertiveness is a form of behaviour; it is not a personality trait. Descriptions such as 'so and so is an assertive person or an aggressive person' are unhelpful because this implies that people only ever behave in one way and this cannot change.

Aggressive behaviour and passive behaviour often come more easily to us because they are instinctive. However, everyone is capable of using different types of behaviour, and at different times different ways of behaving are appropriate. Behaving assertively often feels strange at first and sometimes it is hard to work out whether your behaviour is really assertive. For instance, someone who habitually behaves aggressively may tone this down in an attempt to be more assertive but may just end up being aggressive more politely with a few 'pleases' and 'thank yous' thrown in.

When seeking to understand assertiveness it is often helpful to start by identifying behaviour that is not assertive. When animals are frightened or threatened they fight or run away, or behave submissively in an attempt appease the aggressor.

Passive or non-assertive behaviour
The human equivalent of this is behaving submissively, appeasing the aggressor or even running away. Usually the person does not literally run away but sometimes they do 'shrink into themselves' as a way of getting away from the situation. The person who is behaving passively probably has closed body language and speaks quietly. Passive behaviour includes not saying what you want to, not saying 'no', and avoiding conflict at all costs. The person who is behaving passively can end up doing things they do not really want to and/or becoming a victim.

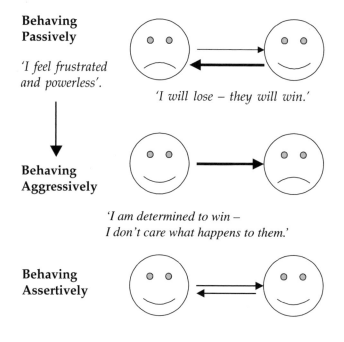

Behaving Passively

'I feel frustrated and powerless'.

'I will lose – they will win.'

Behaving Aggressively

'I am determined to win –
I don't care what happens to them.'

Behaving Assertively

'I want us both to come out of this encounter feeling good about ourselves and each other. I want a win–win situation.'

Figure 4.1   Understanding assertive behaviour

Passive behaviour can lead to aggressive behaviour because underlying a lot of aggressive behaviour is a feeling of powerlessness and frustration.

Aggressive behaviour

When animals fight or are preparing to fight they make themselves larger (for example, dogs raise their hackles), they may make a loud and threatening noise, they usually stare menacingly and sometimes they actually attack. Human aggressive behaviour is often a version of this and tends to include making oneself larger (standing up, pointing, etc.) and making loud noises (shouting, swearing). However, it is important to remember that human aggression does also come in more subtle forms such as sarcasm, ignoring, etc. The thing that all forms of aggression have in common is that during the aggressive encounter the perpetrator seeks to get their own way without respect or regard for the victim.

Underlying both passive and aggressive behaviours are a lack of self-respect; the person behaving passively may have an excessive respect for, or fear of, the other person or may not even be consciously thinking of the other. The person behaving passively feels powerless in getting their way in this interaction. The aggressor is seeking to get their way without regard for the other person, but their aggression may well have its roots in a sense of powerlessness or frustration and may demonstrate an inability to interact in a more mutually respectful way (see Figure 4.1).

People often feel they have no choice about the way in which they behave or that circumstances force them to behave in a particular way. However, behaving differently is likely to engender a different response, which is why learning to behave assertively has become such a powerful strategy for members of groups which have historically been oppressed, such as women and/or people from ethnic minorities.

Assertive behaviour

This includes listening to and seeking to understand others while being open and honest with ourselves. It also includes making decisions having taken into account differing perspectives. The person behaving assertively takes responsibility for their own feelings and behaviour. The consequences of assertive behaviour are that conflict is more likely to be dealt with quickly and effectively, people feel listened to and respected and retain their dignity even in difficult situations.

> Alexis was the manager of a small project within a large voluntary sector organisation. They had staggered through the last financial year on a wing and a prayer and finally she heard the news that the project had lost its funding and was to close. She and the deputy manager would be redeployed but everyone else would lose their job and as they were all on short-term contracts they would not⟳

get any redundancy pay but they would be paid until the end of the financial year whether they stayed on or not. She needed them to stay on for a few weeks to formally close the project down. She called a staff meeting and had to consider how to approach the group.

One option was to say something like: 'I am really sorry, please don't shoot the messenger, the project has to close. It is nothing to do with me. I can't make you, and you will get paid anyway, but please will some of you stay on and close down the project otherwise I am going to be in a real fix.'

'No,' she thought, 'if I take a passive approach like that I am going to get everyone shouting at me, particularly as I still have a job. It sounds like I don't expect anyone to help me out here and I haven't acknowledged their upset at the project closing.'

A second option was to go for the 'no-nonsense' approach.

'Sorry guys, I've done my best but the project is closing. I need you to all stay on until the end of March so that we can close the project down, so at least you will still be paid for a few more weeks and then I will give you a good reference.'

'No,' she thought, 'they deserve better than that; they are all going to be really upset about this, not just for themselves but also for the clients. If I take an aggressive approach like this (especially as I am not telling them the whole truth about the notice period) they will be really upset, I haven't acknowledged their feelings and they will feel bullied.'

So she started the meeting like this: 'You have probably guessed why I have called this meeting. I am really sorry to tell you that despite everyone's best efforts we haven't been able to secure any funding for next year and the project will be closing at the end of March. Even though this news is not unexpected I know you will all be really disappointed; this is all to do with money and nothing to do with the success of the project which you have all contributed to.'

She paused for the news to sink in and for people to make comments.

'I will do everything I can to help you to secure another job. I have to be totally honest with you. Under the terms of your contract you do not have to work until the project closes in order to get paid, and I know you are all really fed up and may want to take some time out to look for another job. But I do need to close the project down properly and I would really appreciate it if you would stay on until the end to help me to do this.'

After the meeting she sat in her office and thought: 'That was awful, I hated having to tell them that the project was closing but at least by taking an assertive approach I let them know I was considering their feelings as well as my own and I think we will all be able to work together to close the project down.'

Later on her PA said that she felt Alexis had hit just the right tone. The staff appreciated that she had been straight with them. They could see that she too was very sad about the project closing but they felt confident that she would keep them all on track giving a good service until the end and that she would do her best to help the staff move on to other work. The whole team decided to stay on for as long as possible to support Alexis, safe in the knowledge that she would support them all through the sadness of closing down, and individually in their job hunting.

Assertiveness in practice

When behaving assertively we always need to think of the other person while making sure that our own needs are being met. We also need to let them know that we have considered them. This is part of the same dance of communication that was discussed in Chapter 2. You only know that your message has been received in the way that you intended by the behaviour of the recipient. One of the key skills needed in order to be assertive is listening. Good listening allows you to find out what the other person's perspective is, and to check that they have received the right message.

Assertive behaviour carries two elements, although in practice these elements often intermingle. **One element of the interaction is about the other person**. This is likely to consist of listening and trying to understand what the other person is saying. In this part of the interaction you will be letting them know that you are trying to understand, or that you have heard what they are saying. **The other element is about you**. This will include you saying what you think and feel and what you would like to happen.

There are no magic words of assertiveness and no magic formulae; however, it is often useful to use what are described in assertiveness training as 'I statements'. This simply means that wherever possible statements should begin with 'I' rather than 'you'. This is because starting a sentence with 'I' demonstrates that you are taking responsibility for your views and feelings. It is also much less confrontational. For example compare *'you really upset me'* with *'I feel upset with what you said.'*

In order to be assertive you need to use all the skills for developing empathetic relationships described in Chapter 2. The body language of assertiveness, like the body language of active listening, is 'open'. That is calm, not defensive and not aggressive. Your voice should also be calm and not too loud or too soft. Eye contact should be sufficient to ensure that the person knows you are listening but not so intense that they feel threatened. It is really important when trying to be assertive to ensure that words and body language are congruent. In fact it often works the other way round. If you can get the body language right it makes it easier to feel assertive and to find the right words. This might involve a self-conscious effort for instance to relax, control your breathing and hence your voice, or to uncross your arms.

Saying 'no'

Sometimes situations arise where the answer to a question is 'no'. Part of maintaining professional relationships and working legitimately (see Chapter 3) is identifying the bottom line, the point beyond which you or the client will not go. In these situations it is useful to be able to say 'no' assertively and clearly. People do not like to hear 'no' but they are much more likely to accept it if the message is given clearly, calmly and assertively. Ambiguous responses which ultimately end up in a 'no' are much more likely to cause frustration and aggression. Many people do not find it easy to make clean, clear statements of refusal. They often fear that saying 'no' will cause offence and or conflict. It is helpful to remember that you are refusing the request not the person.

Saying 'no' needs to be straightforward and simple:

- **It needs to include the word 'no'**. This might seem obvious but in fact people often do not say 'no': they might say things like *'I am really sorry'* or *'I wish that you had not asked me that'*. This might sound like 'no' when you are saying it but to the recipient who does not want to hear 'no', it can sound more like *'if you push me hard enough I can be persuaded'*.

- **One apology**. This shows that you are respecting the other person's point of view. Repeated and abject apologies again start to sound as if you can be persuaded to change your mind.

- **One explanation**. This explains your position or point of view. Again this needs to be clear, to the point, and concise.

- **Open, assertive, non-threatening body language**.

Pro-social feedback

In order to help people to change you have to tell them in a constructive way what you do (or do not) want to encourage about their behaviour. For instance, you might be working with someone who talks about women in a really derogatory way that you find it offensive and irritating. Using assertive pro-social feedback would help you to ask them to behave differently without giving the message that you are judging them as a person; it gives you a strategy for challenging them while avoiding getting into an argument with them.

For example, saying to someone *'you are really sexist and offensive'* is hostile and aggressive and implies that you think they can never change. On the other hand saying something like: *'When you said this morning that women should be either in the kitchen or on their backs I think you were trying to make a joke. However, I found that remark offensive because it makes me feel that you do not respect women and by implication the job that the women in the team are doing here. Please do not say things like that again'* is more likely to provoke a thoughtful response even if the recipient feels uncomfortable with what you say to them.

Pro-social feedback is also a useful strategy for giving people clear and useful praise. You may not necessarily be undertaking major pieces of behaviour change, but in your contacts with clients you will have many opportunities to reinforce positive behaviour and attitudes or discourage negative attitudes, often in a low-key informal way. Pro-social feedback is a skill that will help you to deal with tricky situations that might arise during everyday contact.

Like everything else in pro-social practice this applies to colleagues as well as clients. To give a clear 'thank you' to a colleague, particularly in earshot of a client, is not only a boost to the colleague but also a powerful piece of modelling for the client. Similarly, if you have concerns about a colleague's behaviour pro-social feedback gives you a strategy for assertively addressing this with them (hopefully not in earshot of a client).

However, like many things in pro-social work, feedback sounds like common sense but is not easy to do in practice. In the research done in probation hostels in South Yorkshire (Henry *et al.* 2000) the staff said that learning to give pro-social feedback was incredibly important and effective but it was also the thing that they found most difficult.

Do not forget
Pro-social feedback is used both on behaviour you want to encourage and behaviour that you want to discourage. Researchers in Manitoba,

Canada (Bonta and Rugge 2004) found that probation workers frequently used pro-social reinforcement as a method of influencing change; when offenders reported pro-social activity officers recognised this as desirable and expressed approval. However, they were not so good at responding to anti-social expressions and frequently missed or ignored them, action which could be seen as collusive.

How to give pro-social feedback

Throughout this interaction you will need to retain empathy with the client, using reflective active listening skills and assertiveness to let them know that you are trying to understand their point of view, even if you do not agree with it. You may also want to use motivational techniques (see Chapter 5) to elicit the desire to behave differently from the client.

In order to help you remember the components of pro-social feedback it is described as a series of steps. Some practitioners have found it helpful to have this on a wall, positioned where they can glance at it when talking to clients, as an aide-mémoire.

1 Make sure you both know what you are talking about

Feedback should be given as close to the event as possible. It is often easier to give feedback there and then rather than worry about what you are going to say. Sometimes, however, it is better not to give feedback immediately, for instance you might not want to give it in front of others; you might want to give some thought to what you want to say, or you might want to let someone calm down.

If you cannot give feedback immediately you need to make sure you both know what you are talking about. Be very clear and specific about what you are talking about. For example *'I would like to talk to you about the incident that occurred when you and Billy were arguing in reception'*, rather than *'I want to talk about what happened yesterday'*.

Ideally at this stage the client will be engaged with you in identifying what you are both talking about and if you are lucky they will be able to identify the piece of behaviour that needs to be changed (or reinforced).

2 Make sure you are describing the behaviour not the personality

Behaviour is recognisable and can be changed; describing personality traits is more vague and harder to get a handle on. For instance, if you say to someone, *'I don't like your attitude'*, how are they going to know what you really mean or when their 'attitude' has changed for the better? If, on the other hand, you say *'I don't like the way that you always look away and keep fiddling with your pen when I am trying to talk to you about something serious (because I feel as if you are not listening)'*, you are describing a piece of behaviour, and you will both be able to see when the behaviour has changed.

3 Say what you liked/did not like
Again, if possible, engage the client in identifying the undesirable behaviour, but if they cannot do this, or they do not see why it is undesirable, you will need to spell it out for them. Be clear and straightforward.

4 Explain why you liked/did not like the behaviour (its impact on you/ others)
Steps 3, and 5 provide the pro-social context to what you are saying. In explaining why you did not like something you are identifying why you have made that judgment and in step 5 (below) you are identifying the pro-social behaviour that you are seeking.

Where appropriate start your statement about what you liked/disliked with 'I'. This makes it clear what your pro-social values are, why you are saying what you are saying, and it sounds less hostile and accusatorial than if you start with 'you'.

The suggestion to use 'I statements' is not meant to imply that all pro-social feedback has to be personalised. In many cases you may be telling the client that they have broken a rule or the law; however, the message will still be more powerful if it comes as an 'I' 'statement'. *'I am really concerned because as you know this behaviour breaks the project rules. I am also disappointed because you seemed to be doing so well.'* Compared with *'You have broken the rules and you have undermined all your good work so far'*. The use of 'I' in the first statement reinforces the fact that this is happening in the context of an empathetic relationship.

5 Talk about what might be different
Engage the client in this. You might want make suggestions but listen to their suggestions too.

6 Do not overdo it
Giving feedback is often difficult especially when it is (constructive) criticism. There is always a risk that once you pluck up the courage to give feedback, you will find it hard to stop. Make your point and leave it at that. If there are several things you are unhappy about then it is probably more sensible to deal with just one of them. If you overload people with feedback, critical or positive, they tend to shut down and not hear anything you say.

Examples of pro-social feedback

Behaviour you want to encourage

1 **Make sure you both know what you are talking about.**
   I would like to talk to you about the incident after the group on Wednesday when Pat was refusing to help clear up.
2 **Make sure you are describing the behaviour not the personality.**
3 **Say what you liked/did not like.**
   It really made a big difference that you carried on clearing up, taking no notice of Pat kicking off (not just *'you were very helpful'*).
4 **Explain why you liked/did not like the behaviour (its impact on you/others).**
   I really appreciated the fact that you carried on like that because the others copied you rather than Pat; you were so calm that it calmed the whole situation down. I also appreciated the fact that because you had cleared up I did not have to do your share of the clearing up as well as Pat's.
5 **Talk about what might be different.**
   Not appropriate in this case
   (Be careful not to give praise with one hand and take it away with the other for instance by saying *'You did much better this time but I know you can really do much better than this.'*)
6 **Do not overdo it.**
   In the case of a praise message you might have to repeat it as people often shrug off praise and do not really hear it. So you might say, *'I really mean it, I really did appreciate what you did last night, thank you.'*

Behaviour you want to discourage

1 **Make sure you both know what you are talking about.**
   I would like to talk to you about the incident after the group on Wednesday when you refused to help clear up.
2 **Make sure you are describing the behaviour not the personality.**
   Not *'You were being really stroppy.'*
3 **Say what you liked/did not like.**
   I was annoyed by what happened because we agreed as a group that we would all help to clear up and the quicker it was done, the quicker we could all get away. You were there when we decided that and now you are not sticking to the agreement.
4 **Explain why you liked/did not like the behaviour (its impact on you/others).**
   Also, I was annoyed by all the shouting and I think some of the other group members were quite frightened. When everyone is shouting no one is listening and it doesn't get us anywhere.

5 **Talk about what might be different**.
What are you going to do next time? ...I would like it if you could just get on and help, it does not take very long and we usually all have a laugh together.
6 **Do not overdo it**.
Let's leave it there.

Frequently asked questions about pro-social feedback

I feel stupid going rigidly through these stages
You do not have to work rigidly through the stages. The model is there only to guide you as to what to say. It is important, however, that your feedback includes every element of the model and that you start by making sure that you both know what you are talking about. As you become more familiar with the model it will become easier to use.

The way you do it sounds very blunt
The illustrations are pared down to the bare bones so you probably would not say things just like this. One thing that would make them more effective is to use more motivational techniques (see Chapter 4) so that you are engaging the client more in what they think is right and wrong, good and bad, desirable, undesirable, etc. However, you do need to ensure that at some point you reinforce or emphasise what you think so that there is no danger of the message being lost or of you appearing to collude.

I feel as though I am being patronising when I say all these positive things
In our culture we are not used to giving and receiving praise so it can sound and feel a bit strange. However, we know from research in South Yorkshire Hostels (Henry *et al*. 2002) and research into behaviour change (Bonta 2002) that rewards drive behaviour change, so stick with it. One way of making a praise message sound sincere is to be very clear about the impact the positive behaviour has on you. In the first example above, you might say something like, *'I really don't like being on at you all the time and I have enjoyed this morning and feel much more relaxed than usual.'*

This is all very well in planned one-to-one sessions but most things in the workplace happen quickly and need dealing with there and then
With the proviso that sometimes it is not appropriate to tackle things in public, or when someone is very wound up, you can work through all the elements of the model in a couple of sentences, e.g.:

Chris, you say 'f' and 'c' as every other word. I really find it offensive and if you swear like that in court it will make matters worse for you. Please try to swear less or as a start, try to catch yourself swearing.

How can you use this for the drip, drip, drip of everyday irritations like swearing, without sounding as though you are nagging?
Keep it short, just say what you want to say in a few words, but be persistent and consistent. In other words do not ignore the behaviour a few times and then suddenly start giving feedback on it when you feel more energetic or you can't stand it any more, and then ignore it again because you are getting fed up. This applies to you as a team as well as individuals. If you are not consistent with your feedback, the message will be undermined.

In the staff team we don't talk openly about things we are unhappy about or tell one another when we are pleased with something
Well, now is the time to start. This will be really good practice for the way that you are trying to work with clients and also it is good modelling because sooner or later residents are going to see you giving one another feedback.

Using pro-social feedback to demonstrate non-collusive empathy

Another reason to use pro-social feedback is to avoid any danger of your actions, or lack of actions, being regarded as collusive. If you see, overhear, or are told about something that you think is anti-social (this does not just mean illegal but would also include behaviours and attitudes which are inconsiderate or unpleasant or rude) and do nothing about it, you are giving the message that you approve of it. In other words you are colluding with the attitude or behaviour. As previously discussed Trotter (1999) refers to research that indicates that when workers form empathetic relationships with offenders without reinforcing pro-social expressions and behaviour and discouraging anti-social behaviours and expressions, the risk of reoffending rises. You may not be working with offenders but if you ignore excessive swearing, rude and thoughtless behaviour, discriminatory behaviour or views, you are effectively giving a message that you think these things are all right.

The essence of non-collusive empathy is to separate acknowledgment of the feelings expressed from disapproval of the behaviour.

An example might be:

Client: *Sometimes when I am really angry I just lose control and I find myself smacking them really hard before I know what I am doing.*

Staff member: *I know that sometimes children can be absolutely maddening. I can understand that you get really angry and that you find it hard to control your behaviour, but it is never right to hit them, you are much bigger than them and could really hurt them, and you are also teaching them that the only way to deal with problems is through violence* (acknowledging the strength of feeling but being very clear what you think about the behaviour).

You might follow this up by continuing with a praise message and some optimism.

I think it very brave of you to admit that you hit the children and it makes it much easier for us to work together now it is out in the open. While you are here I am confident that we can do some work both on helping you to control your temper and also other ways of dealing with the problems that lead you to get so angry with them.

Summary

In order to encourage clients to behave differently we have to be able to tell them what we like and dislike about their existing behaviour. We do this within a pro-social context.

Behaving assertively and using pro-social feedback allows us to do this without feeling unduly uncomfortable and in a way that allows the client to hear what we are saying.

Assertive behaviour demonstrates your respect for others and also your respect for yourself.

The aim of assertive behaviour is a win–win situation where everyone comes out of an encounter feeling that they have been listened to and respected.

Assertiveness is not about getting your own way or conceding to another's requests, but about arriving at a decision that has something in it for everyone.

An assertive interaction has within it the following:

- Respect for the other person's point of view. This means listening and demonstrating that you are trying to understand their point of view.
- Respect for your own point of view. This means knowing and saying what you think and feel and want to happen.

Working in a pro-social context it is important sometimes to say 'no'. When saying 'no' we need to:

- Actually say 'no'.
- Give one explanation and one apology (not overdo it).
- Make sure our body language is congruent with the message.

Pro-social feedback: a summary of the model

1 Make sure you both know what you are talking about.
2 Make sure you are describing the behaviour not the personality.
3 Say what you liked/did not like.
4 Explain why you liked/did not like the behaviour (its impact on you/ others).
5 Talk about what might be different.
6 Do not overdo it.

Pro-social feedback can be used to demonstrate non-collusive empathy, because it allows us to acknowledge feelings while commenting on behaviour.

5. Motivating the unwilling client

'When I started the programme I didn't really believe there was any chance of me giving up drugs. I thought I could just pretend because I was trying to get the courts off my back. The staff didn't rush me but they spent a lot of time talking to me and listening to me and slowly but surely I came round to thinking that I really did want to do it and I could do it after all. I know it is going to be really hard and I am going to have to stop seeing a lot of my mates but I am giving it a really good try and I am feeling better already.'

Introduction

While we may have a clear idea about the behaviours that we think are desirable for our clients, they are unlikely to actually change their behaviour and the underlying thinking unless they are motivated to do so. In other words, real change is very unlikely to take place unless clients have both the commitment and the confidence to change. In many settings, particularly in the criminal justice sector, short-term change is maintained by constraint and coercion; however, this change is not necessarily maintained over a period of time. For instance, for those serving short prison sentences in particular, rates of reconviction are high. Around three-quarters of those who have served sentences for burglary or for theft are convicted of a further offence within two years of release (Lewis *et al.* 2003).

Motivational Interviewing was first developed in work with clients with addictions and is based on the concept that change is not an event but a cyclical process. In other words, in order to make a change we go through several stages and if the change is not successful in the short term we can go through the stages again until permanent change is achieved. Most people who have given up an addictive behaviour, like smoking, will tell how they have gone through, what felt at the time, like the same process over and over again until finally they achieved permanent, or at least very long-term change. Miller and Rollnick's (2002, 1991) books, both called *Motivational Interviewing*, have been hugely influential. They introduced their audience to an understanding both of the process of change and also of techniques to move people through these stages towards permanent change.

Although motivational interviewing was developed for work with people with addictions in therapeutic settings there is evidence that it works in other settings too.

Research involving probation officers working with offenders with drug and alcohol dependency problems (Harper and Handy 2002) found that when officers were trained in motivational techniques there was a statistically significant improvement in attitudinal scores of the offenders compared with those supervised by officers who had not been trained in motivational techniques. Ginsberg *et al.* (2002) describe motivational interviewing being used in a variety of criminal justice settings including with offenders where there is no significant alcohol or drug problem.

However, Harper and Handy report that while some officers found motivational interviewing easy to integrate into a probation setting, others found that the time taken to apply the techniques was not always practical in a busy probation setting. Miller and Rollnick's (2002, 1991) books underpin the subsequent developments in motivational work. Fuller and Taylor (2003) developed a simplified version of work to be used in everyday interactions and this was developed further by Fuller (2004) to be used in Probation Approved Premises. This chapter draws on this work as well as that of Miller and Rollnick to introduce simple techniques that can be used in everyday formal and informal interactions with clients.

Pro-social work is about encouraging clients to behave more pro-socially and less anti-socially according to an externally identified set of values (for instance, the laws of the land). Motivational work is about helping the client to develop their inner resources in order to undertake change. However, motivational work is not value-free or entirely client centred and this chapter demonstrates how motivational work can help clients to develop more pro-social behaviours and attitudes.

Why do people change?

Often it is hard to see why people do not change. Why did it take me 20 years to finally and completely give up smoking when for much of that time I knew perfectly well that it was a dangerous, anti-social and expensive habit? Why don't people give up offending when they have been to prison and hated every minute of it and they know that if they reoffend and get caught they will go back for even longer? Why doesn't the drug-abusing mother who dearly loves her children give up drugs even though she knows that continuing drug use puts her children at risk and may result in them being put into care? If fear, punishment, or sheer common sense were enough to make people change then many of us working in welfare, care or criminal justice would be out of a job.

On the other hand we also do see people change against all (apparent) odds. The heaviest smoker I knew stopped smoking without a backward glance when she was planning to get pregnant. The majority of people do stop offending – offending is primarily an act of the under 25s (Farrall 2004). Early reports of Drug Treatment and Testing Orders (DTTOs) show that nearly 30 per cent of people on DTTOs completed their order and substantially reduced their drug use by the end of their orders (Hough et al. 2003). Of this group 43 per cent had not reoffended after two years. This was a substantial improvement on their conviction rate over the previous five years. Although this was criticised by the press as a failure, looking at the client group – chaotic heavy users of illegal drugs supporting their habits by criminal activity – it could be hailed as a major success. Miller and Rollnick (2002) draw on research in the field of addictions and elsewhere to describe the pieces of the puzzle that help us to understand why people do change. The next section draws principally on the work of Miller and Rollnick (1991, 2002) and McNeill (2003).

Change occurs naturally

People grow up, they develop different priorities, support mechanisms and interests and they therefore change. Stephen Farrall (2004) looked at causes of desistance among offenders and found that many people stopped offending when normal life events occurred such as: a change of life direction, leaving school or getting a job, developing long-term relationships, becoming a parent or the break up of the peer group (because other members have grown up and changed too). He also found that people gave up offending because they had got fed up with being arrested or they feared death or injury. This does not explain why some people change their behaviour in response to life experiences and others do not. However, it does suggest that changing life experience signals an opportunity for change which the practitioner might encourage the client to take.

Change after formal interventions mirror 'natural' change

In other words some people change after treatment, counselling or therapy, but the process is very similar to that of people who make the same sort of change without any formal intervention.

The likelihood that change will take place is strongly influenced by interpersonal interactions
Change often takes place after a brief interaction, e.g. brief therapy, professional mentoring, coaching, etc. These interactions and the time span are too short to have resulted in learning complex new skills or personality change, nevertheless change is precipitated that would not happen without the interaction. I finally put steps in place to enable me to write this book after one question from a professional mentor ('what do you really want to do, Sally?'), made me realise how much I wanted to do it and the time was right. The practitioner might well be the catalyst and needs to be alert to this possibility.

Most change takes place early on in 'treatment'
If change is going to take place it usually happens during the first few sessions – lengthy 'treatment' often does not make a lot of difference. (Although sometimes one change needs to be established before a second change can take place. For instance a client may need to develop self-esteem through increasing literacy before they have the confidence to tackle a change in the way they relate to other people.) Continuing interactions may consolidate change and help the client to develop the practical infrastructure to support change; for instance, for drug users to develop a different and drug-free social group.

The way the practitioner relates to the client is a significant determinant of treatment drop out, retention, adherence and outcome
Specifically an empathetic style seems to facilitate change and its absence may deter change. This is an important finding put in the context of the 'brokerage' case management model used in several settings including criminal justice where a case manager (or offender manager) may refer a client to a variety of interventions. It is likely that opportunities to develop motivation in the client are going to be maximised if there is one significant relationship anchoring the interventions.

People who believe they are likely to change do so
People whose practitioner believes they are likely to change also do so. This is supported by Trotter's (1999) findings that optimism is a positive force for change. This is congruent with pro-social modelling being an optimistic, reward-driven model, which encourages practitioners to look out for positive things to encourage, over and above negative things to discourage or sanction.

What people say about change is important
When people say things that indicate they are motivated to change and are committed to doing something they are likely to actually change their

behaviour. When arguments against change (resistance) are developed by the client or provoked by the practitioner, change is much less likely to happen. Both can be influenced by the style of the practitioner. (See the discussion of solution-focused practice in Chapter 2.)

Miller and Rollnick (2002) conclude that motivation is fundamental to change and that the client's motivation to change is a good predictor of outcome. Motivation can be increased by natural events (growing up, taking on new responsibilities, etc.) and also by specific interventions such as a relationship with a therapist, social worker, youth worker or other practitioner. In this case the style of the practitioner and the level of empathetic engagement seem to be particularly important.

What is motivation?

Miller and Rollnick sum this up in the phrase 'ready, willing and able' (2002: 10).

Willing: the importance of change

One important factor is how much the person wants to change. The desire to change often comes from the discrepancy between what is happening and what one wants to happen. Miller and Rollnick refer to self-regulation theory and the concept of discrepancy. If present reality is found to be within desired limits no change is indicated. However, when discrepancy between what is and what is desired increases, the willingness to change increases. However, people are complicated and they may have different things going on in their lives that contradict each other. Every serial dieter will say that their desired state is to be thinner than they are (or perceive themselves to be). Most of them also know that if they ate less they would lose weight. But other forces militate against this happening – for instance, the comfort derived from eating, the social aspects of eating, the belief that it is always better to start a diet on a Monday, the belief that dieting is not healthy and what is really needed is a minor adjustment to current eating habits, etc.

Able: confidence for change

Often people genuinely want to change and can see all the reasons why they should but feel pessimistic about their chances of doing so successfully. The dieters referred to above genuinely want to change but often do not feel confident that they can, especially if they have a history of yo-yo dieting that leads them to believe that they are unable to make permanent change. Self-regulatory theory tells us that if people find a way of changing that they think will work and they believe they can change they will pursue this. However, if they perceive a discrepancy but no way of changing, they will cope with the resulting discomfort by changing their thoughts and feelings instead of the behaviour. This is often described as defensive behaviour. So the potential dieter might think to themselves, 'well, I might be overweight but I am quite fit', or 'I am not going to buy into the cult of thinness, I will be my own person'.

Ready: a matter of priorities

Even when the client feels willing and able to make the required change they may still not be prepared to do it at the moment. For instance, they may feel that they need to concentrate on something else, or that the time is not right.

It is easy as practitioners to see low willingness, low confidence and/ or low readiness as a fixed state. The motivational model, however, sees this as part of the normal human condition and with the potential to change in response to life events including natural developments such as maturing and also outside interventions such as the client–worker relationship. In common with pro-social modelling it is a fundamentally optimistic model which is underpinned by a belief in the infinite capacity of human beings to change. Working with ambivalence, the 'yes, I *want to change, but ...*' dilemma, is one of the fundamental underpinnings of motivational work.

What triggers change?

Many strategies for working with people demonstrating anti-social behaviours are based on the belief that if you make life uncomfortable enough for them they will change. For instance, that if you punish people they will stop doing what they are doing and do something more desirable. We have already looked at the evidence that punishment *per se* does not work (Chapter 3) and that the restrictions of many aspects of the criminal justice system do not change people.

Motivational theory would suggest that the factors involved in change are complicated and often pull against one another. People frequently get confused and immobilised by the complications of all the different factors involved in change. Constructive behaviour change happens when it is connected with something very important, which the client comes to perceive as more important than other factors militating against behavioural change. The task of the practitioner is to provide a safe empowering environment where the client can explore the conflicting factors in order to work out what truly matters.

McNeil (2003) takes an overview of recent studies on desistance (stopping behaviour). McNeil was looking at offending but used studies referring to other types of behaviour too. He described how three factors interact with each other and how it is important for the practitioner to be aware of and utilise these factors.

1 **Age and level of maturity**: Although the practitioner cannot influence the age of the client they can be sensitive to developing maturity and support and encourage this (see Chapter 1 for a discussion of maturity). They may be able to support the client in developing a new lifestyle which is more mature and more pro-social, both through practical help (e.g. finding accommodation) and personal development (e.g. developing thinking skills in a group).

2 **Life transitions and social bonds**: Ties to family, employment or educational programmes create a stake in conformity. In the case of offenders they give them something to lose if they continue to offend. Therefore another way in which the worker can help the client to increase motivation is by helping the client to develop or strengthen social bonds. For instance, by supporting a young person to re-engage in education or helping an adult to find employment.

3 **Subjective narratives, attitudes and motivation**: Qualitative research (Maruna 2000) has demonstrated that changes in people's sense of themselves, reflected in an increasing concern for others and consideration of the future (although these are hard to measure), are also indicators of the likelihood of desistance.

McNeill suggests that an understanding of these three factors enables the practitioner to undertake a thorough assessment and to capitalise on any possibility for change in the client. This might include nudging along change that was potentially going to happen anyway. Research by Trotter (1999), Rex (1999) and others has demonstrated that in an effective client–practitioner relationship the client will be motivated by the worker's interest and concern and be willing to be guided by them as long as they perceive the worker to be genuine.

Motivational work in a pro-social context

The fundamental value of motivational work is that people have the potential to change and this potential comes from within and not from outside. Having said that, it is not an entirely 'client centred' (Rogers 1951) model. Motivational work does have values and goals which, at least in the first instance, may not be intrinsic to the client. For instance, in work with offenders the overarching goal of the practitioner is to stop the client offending; in work with addicts the overarching goal is to stop, reduce or get under control the addictive behaviour. However, unlike a more confrontational approach these goals are not imposed on the client but an understanding of them is gradually drawn out from the client within an empathetic respectful relationship where discomfort with the *status quo* is gradually increased.

The values underpinning pro-social practice have already been discussed in Chapter 3. Motivational work can and does take place within a pro-social context with offenders and others. Underpinning skills are the same for pro-social practice and motivational work: for instance, developing empathy through careful listening and reflection. However, we know from Trotter's work (1999) that in order to encourage pro-social behaviour and attitudes we need more than empathy; in fact empathy without accompanying pro-social reflections can be construed as collusive and can lead to less pro-social behaviour.

Miller and Rollnick (2002) identify the following ethical concerns for the practitioner seeking to work motivationally with a less than fully voluntary client:

- that it might work
- that it might work without the person's direct assent
- that it might work without the person's awareness.

However, they reassure us that motivational work is not some kind of subliminal brain-washing. They say that the motivation to change comes from a discrepancy between what is happening now and what the subject thinks is important. We can help the subject to develop their thinking about what is really important (and we can do that in a pro-social context) but we cannot make the subject change unless they perceive that change to be congruent. In other words, we cannot make people change without them knowing that they are changing.

Sometimes we genuinely believe that we know better than the client does and our role (probation officer, prison officer, child protection worker, etc.) gives us the authority to back this up. For instance, we might believe that stealing is wrong; but the client has justification for it ('my need is greater than theirs', for instance) and is not going to stop stealing just because we say they should. They might stop because we encourage them and help them to change their thinking ('actually it is not right to enter another's property in order to take their possessions') or their priorities ('if I go to prison again I will not see my son grow up') so that there is a greater discrepancy between their behaviour and their values. Clients are not going to be motivated to change unless they have taken, or at least begun to take, different values on board for themselves.

Miller and Rollnick (2002) suggest that one way to deal with the ethical dilemma is to be open and honest about the value base that you are working from, and where appropriate the legal power that you have. In order to influence people towards pro-social behaviour we have to be clear what the rules are and ensure that these are operated fairly and ethically (see Chapter 3).

As this chapter unfolds it will become clear that pro-social modelling and motivations work overlap and merge together in many aspects of practice. The question for many practitioners is the degree to which an understanding of pro-social values and consequent behaviour can and should be elicited from the client, balanced against the degree to which pro-social values and behaviours should be imposed on the client. In practice the two often blur into each other.

Working motivationally is not always the right approach, but it is hard to think of a situation where it is impossible to work pro-socially. Where a quick unequivocal change of behaviour is essential, e.g. in breaking up a fight, or stopping behaviour that is frightening, oppressing or intimidating others, it may be important to be very clear about what you (the worker) want or expect to happen there and then, regardless of what the client wants or thinks. Similarly when telling someone things that are not negotiable such as rules (including laws) it may be important to be very direct. In these examples the worker would (or should) still work pro-socially, specifically in establishing the legitimacy of the rules they are imposing, in modelling appropriate behaviour even in a crisis and in behaving respectfully towards the client.

The following story is designed to illustrate how motivational work and pro-social modelling go hand-in-hand in a hostel setting. I will use various parts of the story to illustrate the rest of the chapter.

A life in a day

Marilee arrived at the hostel at 7.30 in the morning. She was scheduled to work a 24hr shift 9.00–9.00, but she had agreed to come in early and cover for Luke who had to leave early for an appointment.

Luke was supposed to be working until 8.00 but he was ready to leave and was obviously anxious and preoccupied.

'Can you just do a quick handover before you go?' she asked him.

'Sorry, got to go,' he mumbled.

'Hang on, Luke,' Marilee said, 'this isn't like you, you are usually so careful about these kind of things. What's up?'

'Wife's going into hospital,' he said, and before she could say anything else he brushed past her and left.

'Goodness,' she thought. 'He must be worried, but I wish he had taken five minutes to tell me the most important things. Oh well, I suppose I can catch up at the handover meeting at 9.00.' ➲

Ishmael came past; she had never seen him looking so smart.

'Wow, look at you, where are you going?' she said.

'Didn't Luke tell you? I have got a job starting this morning, I was up half the night talking to Luke about it and he said that he would make sure that you were here to see me off.'

'Hey, I am sorry, I didn't know, but well done, where are you working?'

'Homebase,' he said, 'but I know it won't work out and I'll get sacked.'

'No you won't, don't be silly.'

'Yes I will, I always do.'

'This is a hopeless conversation,' thought Marilee, suddenly remembering her motivational work training.

'How much do you want to keep this job?' she asked Ishmael.

'It means everything to me: it will look better when I get to court, it will give me something to do and I can send my parents some money for once.'

'You really want to keep this job, it'll help you when you go to court, it'll give you something to do and you can help your parents,' she reflected.

'Yes' said Ishmael. 'I am the only one of my brothers and sisters who doesn't help my parents out.'

'So helping your parents out is really important to you and to do that you need to make a success of the job. So what are you going to do to make sure you keep the job?'

'Dunno ...' He paused and Marilee waited. 'I need to stick with it, I need to do what I am told and not to even think about nicking anything.'

'And you need to be on time on your first day,' laughed Marilee. 'You had better go, you know exactly what to do, you look great, I'll look forward to hearing all about it tonight.'

Marilee was rushing around as usual when suddenly it was 10.55; she had a key work session booked with George at 11.00. She was dying for a cup of coffee, but she decided to find George and to offer him one rather than just make her own and drink it in front of him. Chatting to George as she made him coffee seemed to get him relaxed and he told her about a visit that he had made to his sister yesterday. As they moved into the key work room Marilee had chance to reflect. George was obviously thrilled to have seen his sister; could keeping in touch with her be the incentive to change his behaviour?

'George,' she said, 'you are obviously really pleased to see your sister: why did you lose touch in the first place?'

George looked visibly shaken by the question and for a minute Marilee wondered if she had gone too far too soon, but the chat over coffee seemed to have made him feel safe enough to talk.

'She hates me drinking, it reminds her of Dad – he was a horrible violent drunk and we all had a terrible time when we were kids. Because of that she has never had a drink. She is married to a really straight man and her kids have all done well for themselves. For years she tried to make me stop drinking and then one day she said that until I stopped drinking she would not see me or speak to me again.'

Rather than jump in Marilee waited and George added:

'I have really missed her, it was great to see her, and I can't bear to think that we will stop seeing each other again.'

'You really care about your sister, and you really want to keep in touch, in fact you can't bear to think that you will stop seeing each other again.'

'No, but we will if I start drinking again, she has made it very clear that those are the rules and I know she means it because she has done it before.'

'You know exactly what the rules are with your sister?'

'Yes. I really don't want to start drinking again for lots of reasons and I certainly don't want to lose Margaret, but she made the rules before and I didn't stop drinking then.'

'You have lots of reasons for not starting to drink again and seeing your sister is one of them. So on this line' (she drew it in the dust on the coffee table) 'this end is very likely and this end not very likely, how likely do you think it is that you will stay off the booze?'

He drew a mark about a third of the way from the 'not very likely' end.

'Can you remember where you drew the line last week?' she said as an aside.

'Here,' he said, laughing and pointing to a spot on the floor right off the table at the 'not very likely' end. 'Progress eh?'

'Certainly is,' said Marilee. 'So what has made the difference?'

'I had kind of forgotten how much I wanted to see Margaret; even though I wrote to her from prison I didn't really expect a reply.'

'So seeing Margaret has really made you want to stick with not drinking.'

'Yes, and also I have been out for two weeks now. It is all very well not drinking in prison, it was easier to get drugs than booze in there but I didn't know that I would be able to manage on the out.'

'So you have been able to stay off booze for two weeks on the out and Margaret wants to see you which you are really pleased about.'

'As long as I stay dry.'

'As long as you stay dry.'

'I am not doing too badly really, am I?'

'You think you are not doing too badly', Marilee reflected.

'Well what do you think?' said George sharply.

Marilee realised that this was the time to slip out of reflection, and reward George for his achievement.

'I think you are doing very well. You look better. You are more cheerful which is nice ... makes you nice to live with, and you sound much more positive.'

George had done a great job of sticking to the point but he now went off into a long story about his nephews and nieces and their children. Marilee listened attentively; she realised that George, who had never had children of his own, was very excited about catching up on all the missed years. Gently she brought him back to focus on his drinking.

'George, you have placed yourself here on the line. Do you think it would be helpful to think about the things that will help you to stay off the booze and the things which might pull you back onto it?'

'OK,' he said doubtfully.

'Here is the balance,' she said, drawing it in on her note pad (they had looked at the decisional balance last week). 'What have you got on this side pulling you towards drinking?'

'Nothing now I am back in touch with Margaret.'

'Nothing,' she said. 'So you are saying that there is no danger at all that you might start drinking.'

'Well ... I miss the flavour, I used to like nice wine and beer before I became a wino, sometimes I think it would be really nice to sit down and have a drink, not to get drunk but to enjoy it, but I know I couldn't do that.'

'Flavour,' wrote Marilee neatly on one side of the balance

'Well I suppose you have to balance that with addiction,' said George.

'Flavour/addiction,' said Marilee quizzically, not sure she understood.

'Flavour would get me drinking, the addiction would keep me there,' explained George.

'OK so you mean the flavour is an attraction but the addiction is a risk?'

'Yes. I can't risk the enjoyment because the addiction would take over.'

'Addiction,' wrote Marilee on the balance.

Twenty minutes later they had drawn a decisional balance. George had identified that the attractions of drinking included enjoyment of drink, socialising with his old friends (although he acknowledged that most of these were dead or inside), and not having to think about anything much. He had also identified that the reasons for not drinking were that he could see Margaret and his extended family, that he felt better physically (he had forgotten what it felt like to feel well). He had also reiterated that he believed he would be back to square one if he had a single drink. The thing he kept saying over and over again was that he had forgotten how important to him his family was and he did not want to lose them again. Marilee reflected this back to him and let him know that she had heard this loud and clear.

After they had talked about some ways in which George could avoid putting himself in the way of temptation (including which residents to stay away from) they finished the session. Before she rushed off to her next task Marilee wrote up her notes. She felt that George now had an incentive to stop drinking but she was worried that he had all his eggs in one basket. If there was a problem with Margaret, or the euphoria of the reunion wore off, did George have anything else to keep him from the booze? Still, she reflected, things were a lot better than they had seemed last week.

The key principles of motivational work

The five key principles of motivational work according to Miller and Rollnick (2002) are to:

1 Express empathy.
2 Develop discrepancy.
3 Avoid argument.
4 Roll with resistance.
5 Support self-efficacy.

Express empathy

Empathy has already been discussed at some length in Chapter 2; in summary it is the ability to put yourself in someone else's shoes and to let them know that you are doing that (or trying to do it). It is not the same as sympathy, which implies that you think and feel the same things and would do the same thing in the same situation. Marilee develops empathy early on with George by chatting to him as she makes him coffee. Although she then asks him a really challenging question 'Why did you lose touch (with your sister) ...?' the empathy they have already established allows George to feel safe enough to reply.

Develop discrepancy
This helps people to see for themselves the inconsistencies between their long-term goals, aspirations and their current behaviour. In Marilee's short conversation with Ishmael he identified that he really wanted to support his parents in the way that his brothers and sisters do and in order to do this he has to make more effort to keep his job.

Avoid argument
Argument breeds resistance to change and is a signal to change strategies. Arguing with a client is imposing your point of view on them rather than enabling them to change their self-perception. Marilee starts to push Ishmael into resistance in her response when he expresses his anxiety about his job. When she backs off and reflects what Ishmael has said, while subtly emphasising the points that she thinks are probably most important to him, it has a much more powerful effect and he comes up with some strategies to help him keep his job with very little prompting. The interaction with Ishmael is an illustration of how motivational techniques can be used informally and briefly.

Roll with resistance
Rolling with resistance engages the client actively in the problem-solving process. Working motivationally can be described as 'listen and nudge'. When a client expresses anxieties, uncertainties or doubts it is important to acknowledge them but listen hard for and then reflect back any hint of movement. Marilee uses a technique borrowed from solution-focused work (see scaling in Chapter 2) to ascertain how likely George thinks it is that he will stay dry. He puts the likelihood as quite low, but Marilee does not respond to the potential negativity. Instead she refers him back to where he was last week and asks him what has made the difference (seeing his sister). She then takes every opportunity to reinforce the importance of his relationship with his sister, which is entirely congruent with his values.

Support self-efficacy
Self-efficacy refers to a person's belief in their ability to carry out and succeed with a particular task and is a key element in motivation for change (Bandura 1977). In motivational work self-efficacy can be developed in several ways. One is by the emphasis on personal responsibility: that

the change can and must come from the subject. Another is by worker optimism that is often demonstrated by being solution-focused rather than problem focused (see Chapter 2). In the context of pro-social work self-efficacy can sometimes be increased by actually helping the client to develop new skills by coaching and giving feedback, or making learning opportunities available. Often there might be a chicken and egg situation: for instance, a client with low levels of literacy might feel more confident and able to tackle many changes in their life if they learned to read and write. However, if they fear that they are bound to fail if they try to learn to read and write they may not even be prepared to try. The task for the worker might be to help the client to get to the state of mind where he or she is prepared to risk trying to learn to read and write and then to build on the confidence developed from that experience.

The key skills of motivational work

According to Miller and Rollnick (2002), the key skills of motivational work are:

1 Affirming.
2 Listening.
3 Using open questions.
4 Summarising reflectively.
5 Supporting change talk and self-motivating statements.

These key skills are closely related to those to develop empathy and rapport that are essential for working pro-socially which are identified and discussed in Chapter 2. Motivation work is a specific area within the context of pro-social work and requires an extremely high level of sensitive communication.

Affirming
Trotter (1999, 2004) and others have identified how important it is to reward people for behaviours that you want more of rather than punish them for the things that you want less of. Many clients may have heard many negative messages about themselves and very few positive ones; in this case it is very important to ensure that the praise message is clear and specific.

Marilee's praise to George in the middle of the key work session, 'I think you are doing very well. You look better. You are more cheerful which is nice... makes you nice to live with, and you sound much more positive' is very clear and specific.

Even apparent criticisms can contain affirmations. Marilee says to Luke when he is rushing out without doing the handover. *'Hang on, this isn't like you, you are usually so careful about these kinds of things.'* The implication being that his current behaviour is a deviation from the norm.

Listening

Listening is a crucial skill for gaining a real understanding of the person. Good listening enables us to establish rapport, to understand the way others are looking at the world, and to find ways of communicating with them. As Fuller says (2004: 15) 'many of the people that we work with may have had a good talking to in the past but not a good listening to'.

Open questions

The quest in motivational work is to elicit 'change talk' and then affirm and reinforce it (listen and nudge) and some questions are more likely to elicit 'change talk' than others. For instance, the question 'what worries you about your behaviour?' is likely to help the client become aware of the discrepancy between what they are doing and what they want or think they should be doing. On the other hand the question 'what stops you changing?' is more likely to elicit problem focused and/or resistant answers. In motivational work an excess of questions, even open questions, can provoke resistance so questions should only be used when essential and should be balanced by reflections.

Marilee asks Ishmael *'How much do you want to keep this job?'* She then follows this twice by reflecting everything Ishmael has said about the reasons he wants to keep the job, hence encouraging Ishmael to make self-reinforcing statements. By the time she asks him *'what are you going to do to make sure you keep the job?'* he has reminded himself of how important it is and tries hard to think of something positive. This encounter is a very short one as Ishmael is leaving; if Marilee had had more time she would probably have spent much longer reflecting Ishmael's statements of his reasons for keeping the job before moving to another question.

Summarising and listening reflectively

Reflective listening makes a guess at what the person means and reflects this back as a statement, not a closed question. At the beginning of the key work session with George, Marilee repeatedly reflects what George has said. Each time he responds by adding more positive reasons that he has to change and Marilee reflects these back to him again. Marilee does not add any new information, it all comes from George. If she had responded with a closed question, for instance *'So are you saying that you now want to keep off the booze because you want to keep in touch with your sister?'* his response could well have been *'Yes, but ...'* which then has the potential for him to start building up, reasons why he might not succeed. As it was George clearly felt that Marilee was understanding and hearing him and he was able to build up his own reasons, for himself, why he should stay off alcohol.

Reflections can be of what you think the other person is **feeling** *'so you feel'*, of what you think they **mean** *'so you mean ...'* or of what you think you **heard** *'so you are saying ...'* Tone of voice is very important because as long as the reflection sounds like statement, not a question, if what you reflect does not correlate with what the person thinks they meant they will tell you. Often a slightly naive tone of voice will help both you and the client work out what they mean. When Marilee and George are constructing the decisional balance he says he has to balance the flavour with addiction. She responds by repeating what he said *'flavour/addiction'* and he immediately elaborates on this, increasing Marilee's understanding and also his own.

Reflections can also be used to 'listen and nudge' as the emphasis in the reflection can be on the things that will move the conversation in the right direction, such as discrepancies or change talk. The decision on what to 'nudge' is underpinned by the values of the worker. In the very brief conversation with Ishmael, Marilee twice reflects back to him what he has said about the importance of his relationship with his parents. Marilee, working in a probation hostel, is clearly operating in a pro-social context and she is 'nudging' Ishmael towards becoming motivated to get and keep a job and George towards giving up drinking.

Roadblocks (see Chapter 2) such as arguing, contradicting, etc. get in the way of reflective listening and invoke resistance. Marilee starts her discussion with Ishmael with a roadblock when he tells her that he thinks he will get sacked and she says *'don't be silly'* he immediately retorts *'yes, I will, I always do'.* Fortunately she realises what is happening and moves to a more reflective way of interacting.

Supporting change talk and self-motivating statements

The skills described above are all used to highlight a sense of ambivalence about the current situation, to generate a sense that the *status quo* is not what the client wants to continue in their life. They are used to develop in the client a desire to change something in order to resolve that ambivalence.

Fuller (2004) describes a series of stages through which the client needs to be 'nudged':

1 Acknowledging there is more of a **problem** with their behaviour than they originally thought.
2 Recognising that they are **concerned** about this.
3 Developing the **intention** to do something about this.
4 Developing **optimism** that they can do something.

At this stage specific goal setting and action planning is undertaken.

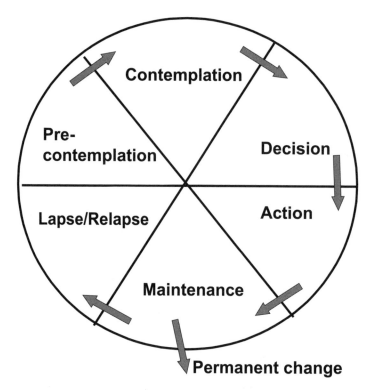

Figure 5.1 The cycle of change (adapted from Miller and Rollnick 1991: 15)

The cycle of change

An underpinning belief of motivational work is that change is not something that might happen but a process influenced by our own desires, values and priorities at any moment in time. Motivational work helps us move people through that process.

Prochaska and DiClemente (in Miller and Rollnick 1991) researched behavioural change in the field of addictive behaviours and developed a six-stage model of the cycle of change. This model is useful in many different areas, not just addictive behaviour, when looking at change and how to facilitate it. For instance, I have used it with managers to help them to look at why people are not motivated to perform and how to encourage them to do so (see Chapter 9); with group workers to help them to understand why people are not engaging in activities and what they can do to help, and with many people working with offenders.

This model is deliberately drawn as a wheel or circle symbolising the fact that change is a process and it is normal for people to go through the process several times. Relapse is a normal stage of the process. Prochaska and DiClemente found that smokers ordinarily went round the wheel between three and seven times before quitting for good.

It is essential that we understand where people are on the cycle of change as different skills and strategies are needed for working at different stages and to help people to move to subsequent stages or to prevent lapsing.

Pre-contemplation

This is the earliest stage of change and people in pre-contemplation either do not recognise their behaviour as problematic or do not see any prospect of it changing so they are unwilling to try.

The words that clients use are usually a clue as to where they are on the cycle. The language of pre-contemplation might include:

- 'I don't have a problem.'
- 'I don't care.'
- 'I am not going to change.'
- 'I can't change.'
- 'It is not my problem, it is someone else's.'

Many clients brought to our attention against their will for instance, through the courts – may not see the need to change and could be described as being in pre-contemplation.

The aim when working with people in pre-contemplation is to build discrepancy between where they are and the values and goals they consider important, using all the skills described above. Often the client may feel hopeless and that there are no choices available for them and one strategy may be to explore choices. People in pre-contemplation can be discouraging to work with but as DiClemente and Velasquez say (in Miller and Rollnick 2002: 208):

> It is erroneous to believe that pre-contemplaters don't ever change and there is nothing we can do. They can be coaxed, encouraged, informed and advised. We cannot make pre-contemplators change but we can motivate them to move towards contemplation.

It is important not to rush people in pre-contemplation before they are ready. Probation service targets mean that many people are referred to Accredited Programmes (structured group work), to address their offending behaviour. Research into attrition (why people do not complete the programme) by Kemshall and Canton (2003) suggests that if people are not at the right stage – for example, if they do not see their offending behaviour as a problem and therefore cannot see the point of attending a group – they are much more likely to drop out.

91

Contemplation

In the contemplation stage, a person is beginning to acknowledge that they have a problem and to think seriously about doing something about it. They might be weighing up the pros and cons of their existing lifestyle. They may be a long way from actually making a commitment to change and it is important not to rush them at this stage. The language of contemplation might include:

- 'I am beginning to wonder.'
- 'I am not sure if I can go on like this.'
- 'I am not happy with this.'
- 'What help is available?'

The task of the worker is to help the client explore their ambivalence and balance up the potential risks and benefits of change. It is also important for people in contemplation to receive accurate information about the implications of their choices so (in a pro-social context) the worker needs to be clear about the rules and requirements of the supervisory arrangement and the consequences of breaking those rules. This is giving the client useful information when considering their choices. It is also acting legitimately in that it is being open about the value base within which you are working.

Decision

This is the point at which the person has decided to act in the near future. At this stage they need to develop a plan which will work for them.

The language of decision might include:

- 'I want to do something about this.'
- 'Please can you help me?'
- 'I am certain that I cannot go on like this.'

The task of the worker is to help the client plan how they are going to undertake the change and also to make a solid realistic assessment of the difficulties they might encounter along the way and to develop strategies to deal with these. It is important not to confuse decision with action. The client may have made up their mind that they want to change, in other words they are **ready and willing**, but they may still need help to believe that they are **able** to change and to leap into action.

Action

This is the point where the behaviour change actually starts. This is a busy period but it is also a time when the client may feel very vulnerable and scared. Sometimes the reality of entering the action stage can be almost overwhelming, for instance, a drug abuser in withdrawal may feel very ill. A person who has left an abusing partner may feel very lonely. It is important to recognise just how fragile the client may be at this stage.

It is usually obvious that someone is in the action stage. The worker has several tasks here: (i) to acknowledge and affirm (reward) the behaviour change; (ii) to provide practical help if needed to get the client through the early stages of the change; and (iii) to help the client make a realistic assessment of problems they might encounter and strategies that might help them. In Marilee's discussion with George about his drinking she helped him to see what might put him at risk of starting to drink again (including residents who might be a bad influence) and to develop strategies to manage this risk.

Maintenance

Maintenance is the final stage in the process of change and is where the change becomes consolidated and made long term. According to the model of change as a cycle this is not a static state and work still needs to continue to maintain motivation, because change takes a very long time to become fully established.

Relapse

It is often hard work to keep up change especially if the circumstances do not support it. An example might be a young person trying to re-engage in school when their peers do not think school is 'cool'. After the initial energy and excitement of the change have worn off it may feel like very hard work. Something in the person's life may change which makes sustaining the change more difficult. In George's case he might end up being housed some distance from his sister and then her positive influence might be lost. Often relapse occurs because ambivalence still remains: sometimes people engage on a process of change because of an external threat (e.g. imprisonment) without developing the intrinsic motivation to change and this will make it especially difficult for them to maintain the change. Sometimes relapse occurs because the client has moved through the stages too fast. One of the tasks of the worker is to respond positively when a client expresses enthusiasm for change while still ensuring that the client has explored their feelings thoroughly at each stage.

With a good working relationship the client may tell the worker that they feel vulnerable to relapse and ask for help or they may hint that they are feeling vulnerable: *'I am feeling a bit low this week'*. The task of the worker will be to help them to revisit the reasons that they made the decision to change in the first place and to rebuild their confidence (self-efficacy) to engage with the change. Whether the person has actually relapsed or not the worker should revisit the stages of the cycle with the client. At the same time the worker needs to acknowledge that change is hard, and affirm (reward) the client's achievements so far and work with remaining ambivalence. If the person has relapsed the cycle model and clinical evidence would suggest that all is not lost, as people often do not return to the pre-contemplation stage: having experienced change once they will try again.

One other thing to remember is that people might be in different stages of the cycle in different elements of their life. For instance, drug users who commit crime to support their habit sometimes manage to reduce their drug use sufficiently that they can give up crime.

Fleet and Annison (2003) suggest that although motivational interviewing is seen as a lengthy process, in the right circumstances it can be delivered as a brief, even single session or intervention. Examples might be to strengthen commitment to compliance and participation in a planned intervention, or as a rescue intervention at signs of declining motivation or diminishing sense of self-efficacy. Marilee's discussion with Ishmael shows how motivational techniques can be used in a brief intervention.

The decisional balance

Change is not a straightforward process and for most people change is not unequivocally a good thing. When we change we lose things as well as gain things and this is one of the reasons that change is difficult. A decisional balance (Miller and Rollnick 1991) is a way of exploring the elements of clients' ambivalence in order to tip the balance in favour of change.

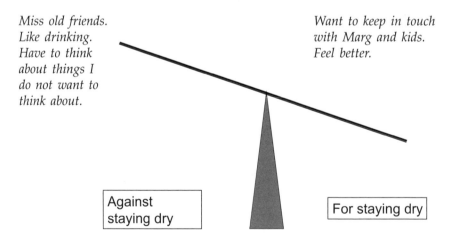

Miss old friends.
Like drinking.
Have to think
about things I
do not want to
think about.

Want to keep in touch
with Marg and kids.
Feel better.

Against staying dry

For staying dry

Figure 5.2 George's decisional balance (adapted from Miller and Rollnick)

Marilee and George drew a decisional balance. On one side of the balance are the things that militate against change or that will make change difficult, the costs of changing and the benefits of the *status quo*. On the other side are the things that will help the change, the costs of the *status quo* and the benefits of change. George's balance might look something like Figure 5:2.

Marilee can now explore each of these factors with George in order to help him tip the balance in favour of staying dry. For instance they both recognise how important his relationship with Margaret is (although this has not stopped him drinking in the past) and George will need to keep reminding himself of this. However, it is also clear that he is attracted to being with the 'drinking crowd' and in a hostel such a crowd is going to be very easy to find so George needs to develop strategies for avoiding this group.

The decisional balance can be used at various stages in the change process from contemplation, where it can be used primarily to explore ambivalence about changing at all, to maintenance where it can be used to explore remaining ambivalence and risks to maintaining the change (and how to manage these). It is not usually used in pre-contemplation because the client is yet to acknowledge more than a grain of ambivalence.

Summary

Motivational strategies can be used to help clients develop more pro-social behaviour and attitudes. Clients are unlikely to change unless they are motivated to do so; in other words they need to be ready, willing and able. This commitment and confidence has to be internalised; external coercion is unlikely to be enough to engender permanent behaviour change. However, working in a pro-social context, clarity about consequence may be one factor that encourages change.

Change is not a static condition but is a process through which people can move several times before making permanent change.

Change is a natural process, people change because of normal processes such as growing up, falling in love or becoming a parent. Change that takes place after intervention mirrors normal change, that is, it is the same kind of change that takes place for others without treatment. Understanding the factors in people's lives which might strengthen their motivation to change (including stopping or desisting from certain behaviours) is important because this might be a cue to 'give them a nudge'.

The relationship with the practitioner is very important; an empathetic style seems to facilitate change. Practitioner optimism including solution-focused practice is also important.

Motivational work is an important element of pro-social practice, and is often based on values external to the client (for instance, crime is wrong, drinking to excess is undesirable). Motivational work seeks to draw from the client an internalised understanding of the goals identified. It does not seek to and cannot force a client to change against their will.

Whereas it is always possible to act pro-socially motivational work is not the right solution in every situation. Sometimes a more directive approach is appropriate, for example, when establishing and enforcing rules.

The key principles of motivational work are:
- Express empathy.
- Develop discrepancy between long-term goals and aspirations and their current behaviour.
- Avoid argument because argument breeds resistance.
- Roll with resistance.
- Support self-efficacy.

The key skills of motivational work are:
- Affirming.
- Listening.
- Open questions.
- Summarising and listening reflectively.
- Supporting self-talk and self-motivating statements.

The cycle of change: a very useful model in motivational work is Prochaska and DiClemente's cycle of change, which shows us that people move through stages in the process of change. It is very important to recognise what stage people are at as it is counterproductive to use the wrong intervention strategy for the wrong stage. For instance, action planning with someone who is in pre-contemplation or contemplation is very unlikely to engender change.

The decisional balance is a useful tool for exploring ambivalence.

6. Practical ways of helping people to change

'My previous social worker kept saying that he was concerned about the way in which I interacted with the kids. I never really understood what he was on about. This one has actually taught me to play with them, I know it sounds stupid but my mum was too ill to play with me so I suppose I never really learned how to do it before.'

Introduction

You have been working with your client for a while, you have formed an empathetic relationship with them, you have clearly sorted out your respective roles and you are trying hard to be positive and rewarding in your interactions with them. Your values are very clear to yourself and the client and they like and respect you, see you as a role model and want to be more like you. They know that you are encouraging them towards more pro-social patterns of behaviour. You have helped them become motivated and to engage in the change process. Despite all this they still do not change. Why is this?

Change is a difficult and complicated process for adults. Any one of us who has tried to eat differently, take up an exercise regime or give up smoking can testify to this. Even when we know exactly what we want to do, are convinced that it is the right thing and even know how we should do it, anything can push us off the path of good intentions.

For some of our clients change may be even more difficult. They may not perceive themselves as having any history of successful change and therefore may not believe in their ability to change. They may be so anxious that their feelings dictate the way in which they behave. They may have learned skills and abilities that served them very well in one setting but which they cannot transfer successfully to another. They may have forgotten skills (after a long spell in prison, for instance), or they may never have learned the skills in the first place and they simply do not know what to do.

This chapter discusses the various ways in which we can help people through the process of change.

Small steps

One way we can help people to change is to encourage them to see change as a series of small manageable steps and support and encourage (reward) them through each step. If they take a small step and succeed, that will motivate them to take the next step and the next. If they take a step and do not succeed they have not lost the whole endeavour but can go back and have another go at taking the first step.

> Mary was a participant on an assertiveness course. When the trainer asked a general question to the group about why we find it hard to say 'no' to people, she cried and said she had never said 'no' to anyone, and everyone – including her family and even the children in the Sunday School that she helped to run – walked all over her. A little later she and the trainer worked with a small group where they were doing a role-play of a situation in which they wanted to say 'no'. Mary wanted to have a go but the whole role-play was more than she could manage. The trainer suggested that she just tried saying the word 'no' firmly and clearly. She could barely whisper the word but the trainer, and the rest of the group, congratulated her warmly for trying. She had several attempts, each time the 'no' got fractionally louder and the group all congratulated her. After a few minutes the trainer thought that she had had enough and another member of the group did their role-play. Later in the day Mary was in another group, doing another role-play and the trainer overheard her saying quite firmly and clearly (in role), 'No, I am sorry but I am not prepared to do that'. Taking that first small step had given her the confidence to take a much larger step later on in the day.

Help them to relax

Often offenders and others get themselves into trouble because they are anxious and cannot manage their feelings. For instance, people in stressful situations such as a court appearance or a tricky interview behave in a way which is perceived as inappropriate and disrespectful, such as giggling. Paradoxically this is not because they do not realise the seriousness of the situation, but because they know it is serious and their anxiety overwhelms their ability to think about how they ought to behave.

Sometimes one of the most useful things that we can do is to help clients to become aware of their feelings and to manage those feelings so that they can behave more appropriately. The following is a simple relaxation technique that can be taught in a few minutes. It can sound a bit silly when you are trying to describe it to someone so it is important that you demonstrate as well as tell.

A simple relaxation technique

Ask the client if they know how to take a deep breath (they probably do not).

Ask them to stand up, describe to them (using gestures as well as words) how the lungs come right down to the diaphragm (bottom of your ribs just above your stomach) and unless we are sports people we often do not use most of our lungs.

Ask them to put their hands, with fingertips touching on their stomach, about a hand's width below the diaphragm and take a really big breath, sucking air down as far as they can into their stomach: their fingertips should part a fraction. You need to do this as well and show them what you mean. (Another way to do this is to ask them to lie on the floor with a book on their stomach. The book will go up and down as they breathe.)

Do not spend too long on this; some people find it very hard, but the important thing is that they are taking the time to try.

After they have had a go, get them to try and link taking a deep breath to releasing tension, so talk them through a sequence, for example:

'Take a deep breath ... Hold it (not for too long!), let it go slowly and as you breathe out let your shoulders relax, let your tension blow away with the breath.'

Repeat a couple of times then introduce the idea that we all hold tension in different parts of our body: ask the client where they feel tension – you might have to help them with this as they may not be aware of their own feelings. Prompts might be:

'When I am tense I find myself clenching my teeth, so if I am going to let go of my tension I have to let go of my jaw muscles. You might find yourself clenching your stomach muscles/neck/fists, etc.'

99

Repeat the breathing exercise and get the client to practise relaxing places in their body where they feel tense. (Do not get people taking more than two or three breaths without a pause to breathe normally otherwise they will feel dizzy.)

Thus far, you both will have been taking very exaggerated breaths, but now get them to repeat the same process but more subtly.

Link this learning to potential problems by saying something like:

> *When you are in court and feeling very nervous how do you think you could use this to help you feel a bit better?*

People often say that they would hardly be likely to stop and take a huge breath; remind them that this can be done much more subtly and ask them to practise taking a breath and letting go of tension during the following days.

Note: In a cognitive behavioural context this exercise is literally about helping people to understand the link between thoughts, feelings and behaviour. It works well because the 'hands on' approach helps clients to physically feel their feelings.

An alternative exercise

In some settings, for instance when working with sex offenders, workers feel that it is inappropriate to do anything that draws attention to their (the worker's) body. An alternative exercise might be to get the client to count to ten while breathing out and letting go of tension in their body. This loses the modelling and showing aspect as the worker does not do it alongside the client, but it does avoid embarrassment.

Showing as well as telling

Clients often do not undertake new behaviours because they do not know how to rather than because they do not want to. This may be because no one has ever showed them, or explained, how to do something. I have already described pro-social modelling as parenting for grown-ups and if clients experienced poor or disjointed parenting they may have gaps in their skills that the rest of us take for granted.

When teaching children new skills parents have to show them what to do and often do it with them. Many skills are difficult to learn solely from verbal instructions. If you are trying to teach a skill that is completely outside the realms of the client's experience, however obvious it might seem to you, you are unlikely to be able to teach them by simply telling them. Also people have different learning styles and ways of processing information (see Chapter 8) and for many people a simple explanation will go straight over their heads. The relaxation technique above is a good example. It is much easier to grasp the idea of breathing deeply into your diaphragm and relaxing various bit of your body if someone is showing you as well as telling you.

Anyone involved in residential work or who spends a lot of time in close proximity with groups of clients will say that good personal hygiene is a vital pro-social skill. How to keep ourselves and our clothes clean is a skill that most of us learn gradually as children from our parents. Adults who have not learned this are not going to achieve a body-odour free existence just because someone tells them to go and have a shower. I am not suggesting that workers need to get into the shower with them – that would be taking role modelling a little too far – however, with a mixture of mime and explanations the client needs to have the steps of showering or bathing, including washing all parts of the body demonstrated. Also how to use deodorant, how to wash their clothes, and how frequently to do this, etc.

Another example might be teaching someone to say 'please' and 'thank you'. The worker may have to point out that saying these words is part of the common courtesy that makes it easier to get on with others. The worker may also have to point out when it is appropriate to use these words and model it themselves whenever the opportunity arises.

Returning to the parallels between pro-social modelling and parenting, it is important to remember how long it takes a child to learn some behaviours even with the constant loving reinforcement of their parents. It is therefore going to be that much harder for an adult who may have to unlearn old habits as well as learn new behaviours. It is also important that when we are supporting clients through changes we form empathetic relationships with them and constantly reward (reinforce) their **efforts** as well as their **successes**.

Be positive and optimistic and use solution-focused language

Working in a solution-focused way (as discussed in Chapter 2), is often a helpful way to move clients from being overwhelmed by problems towards beginning to identify solutions. Trotter (1999: 28) talks about how important it for workers to believe the client can change and to form a relationship such that the client believes the worker can help.

For the worker to be credible they need to balance optimism with realism, otherwise there is a danger that the client will feel that the worker is setting them too high a target.

> Colette was sent to a Young Offender Institution after a series of shoplifting offences committed over a short period of time. She was in the middle of her GCSEs and her teachers in the prison quickly realised that she was very bright and academically able. One teacher in particular was excited by the possibility of teaching such a bright girl; she also recognised that the disruption in her education at such a crucial time could be disastrous for Colette. This teacher formed a good relationship with Colette and was soon encouraging her to sit her GCSEs in prison. Colette liked the teacher and was flattered by her faith in her. However, she had a lot to cope with in prison and felt that she would be unable to cope with the amount of studying she needed to do. She could not articulate this anxiety so she became so disruptive in the education centre that the possibility of doing GCSEs was in danger of being withdrawn.
>
> Fortunately the teacher realised what was happening. She did not give up on Colette but scaled down her expectations. Colette responded well to the fact that the teacher continued to believe in her, and settled down. In the event she passed five GCSEs and this was sufficient to get her a place in her local sixth form college on release.

A staged model for helping people to change their behaviour

Like the steps for pro-social feedback (Chapter 4) this model (adapted from Gast and Taylor 1998) is designed as a reminder of the stages to help people to change. It also could be put up on a wall as an aide-mémoire.

Stage 1   Identify the specific behaviour that needs to change
Workers need to help clients to identify specific problems that they want to work on. This might include behaviour that they want or need to change: offending behaviour or something that leads to offending behaviour such as an inability to say 'no'. It might include behaviour that the client has not learned how to do, for instance arranging an appointment on the phone.

Identifying what you are going to work on is very important; do not be tempted to rush into the next stage too quickly. It is important that the client feels committed to the process and shares the definition of the problem. Workers need to build a good rapport by listening actively and using appropriate questioning techniques.

A motivational and solution-focused approach would be to ask what would be different if they achieved their first aim. This also has the advantage of giving the client something to aim for. However, beware of letting the client identify goals for themselves that seem so big as to be completely unattainable, such as *'I would like to become a law abiding citizen, happily married, with three kids and a good job'*. In this case you would be well advised to ask what would be a good first step that told them they were on their way to their life goal.

Stage 2 Break down the targeted behaviour into the smallest possible parts
Having identified the gaps, the targeted behaviour needs to be broken down into the smallest possible parts so that each part can be addressed and worked on in achievable sections, giving the client something manageable to work on.

Using the example of the person who grins inappropriately when nervous, the small part of this might be the grin and within this getting in touch with the aspects of the grin, e.g. what the face muscles feel like when grinning and not grinning. In this example you might want to try and help the client connect his or her feelings to the behaviour. If they are grinning because they feel nervous, help them to get in touch with what 'nervous' feels like and how to manage those feelings (e.g. deep breathing, relaxation, etc.)

Stage 3 Identify the errors in thinking patterns that are leading to inappropriate behaviour
The reasons that people behave the way they do are many and various but often we can identify an error in the way people are thinking that leads them to behave in a certain way. For instance, they might be misinterpreting other people's motives, they might only be looking at things from their own point of view or they may be avoiding something that they find uncomfortable.

You can challenge errors in thinking by:

- Increasing self-efficacy through motivational work (see Chapter 5).

- Increasing self-awareness and ability to put self in others' shoes through group work programmes, key work, etc.

- Encouraging them to see things from other people's point of view: *How do you think you would feel if you had your purse stolen out of your bag when you were out shopping with your child?*

- Normalising: *It is perfectly normal to feel nervous if you are going to a job interview; I was sick before my interview for this job.*

- Demonstrating optimism: *I am really confident that if we work together we can help you to learn how to tackle this.*

- Challenging beliefs: *What makes you think that the man was about to hit you?*

Stage 4 Work with them to identify what a competent performance might look like

This process is often a mixture of **asking** the client what they are aiming for (perhaps by getting them to reflect on role models they have) and **showing** them through mini role-plays. Remember, when you are asking someone to do something outside their realm of experience you will need to **show** them how to do it as well as **tell** them. It is important not to be too brilliant at it; it is much less scary to learn from someone who is modelling coping, rather than excellence. In practice this means a negotiation between the client and the worker where the worker is never dogmatic. You might be saying things like, *'how about trying this?'* or *'I think I might do this; do you think it might work for you?'*

Stage 5 Slowly build up to more complex behaviour

When the client is feeling more confident about one or two pieces of behaviour encourage them to link them together. Often when one or two things feel better people are encouraged and other things start to fall into place.

Give them lots of opportunity to practise. Remember they may be unlearning the habits of a lifetime so do not encourage too high expectations too quickly. Make sure that you provide lots of encouragement, support and rewards.

Stage 6 Encourage the transfer of new behaviour to different settings

Remind the client that the skills they have learned in one setting can be transferred to another. For instance, if they have learned to control their anxiety and communicate to the Job Centre Plus official what they need to know, they can use the same skills when they need to visit the doctor.

Stage 7 Gradually reduce explicit reinforcements

Learning to cope without reinforcement is an important stage, but if you are encouraging the client to do something that they find really challenging reduce the reinforcement slowly and do not forget that they might need reminding of just how much they have achieved.

Stage 8 Talk about dealing with difficulties/relapse/new situations

Talk through with the client what they are going to do if the newly learned behaviour does not work for them. Acknowledge the fact that behaviour change is difficult and it will not all happen at once, but also demonstrate optimism that it is possible. Work with them to identify small realistic targets and to identify where and how they are going to use their new skills.

An example using the staged model

1 **Identify the specific behaviour that needs to change**.
   Did you know that when you are in court you grin so that makes you look as if you don't respect the court?
2 **Divide the targeted behaviour into the smallest possible parts.**
   Can you feel the muscles in your face when you smile?
3 **Identify the errors in thinking patterns that are leading to inappropriate behaviour.**
   I think that you are so scared that you do not know what you are doing, but the magistrates are not out to 'get you' – they want to see evidence that you are listening to what they are saying and are taking them seriously.
4 **Work with them to identify what a competent performance might look like**.
   They want to see you looking serious. Like this ... do you want to try? ... can you feel the muscles in your face and feel the difference?
5 **Slowly build up to more complex behaviour.**
   Take a deep breath and let your shoulders go, now try and look serious again. Great.
6 **Encourage the transfer of new behaviour to different settings**.
   Can you think of another situation where this might be useful?
7 **Gradually reduce explicit reinforcement.**
8 **Talk about dealing with difficulties/relapse/new situations.**
   What are you going to do if you feel yourself start to panic and lose control in court?

Although this model works best in a safe and calm environment where learning can be developed over a period of time, the principles can be used for 'in the corridor' or 'on the wing' conversations too.

> *So you are worried about phoning your girlfriend because you never manage to say the right things in the short time available. Let's have a think about it; with a bit of help I am sure you will feel more confident.* (Optimism.)
> *What happens when you phone her?* (1)
> *What could you do before you even pick up the phone?* (2)

> *Are you sure she wants to pick a fight, she seems pretty fond of you when*
> *she comes to see you? (3)*
> *What do you really want to say, what is the important message that you*
> *want to get over to her? (4)*
> *Go on then, have a think about it before you phone tonight, good luck.*

Note: Chapter 9 contains a case study using this model for manager–staff interactions.

Summary

Sometimes despite our best efforts clients do not seem to make much progress, there are all sorts of complex reasons for this that we need to take account of including the fact that if the change is outside the realms of their experience they may simply not know what to do.

There are various strategies that we can use to help them to change including:

- Taking small steps.
- Helping them to relax and manage their feelings because anxiety often causes inappropriate behaviour and/or gets in the way of behaviour change.
- Taking them through a step-by-step process, working alongside them, and showing as well telling them what they might do.
- Being positive and optimistic.
- Working with the client's description and analysis of the behaviour that they want to change.

It is often useful to use a simple staged model for helping people to change their behaviour:

1 Identify the specific behaviour that needs to change.
2 Divide the targeted behaviour into the smallest possible parts.
3 Identify the errors in thinking patterns that are leading to inappropriate behaviour.
4 Work with them to identify what a competent performance might look like.
5 Slowly build up to more complex behaviour.
6 Encourage the transfer of new behaviour to different settings.
7 Gradually reduce explicit reinforcement.
8 Talk about dealing with difficulties/relapse/new situations.

7. Taking a systematic, pro-social, collaborative approach to problem solving

'In the first session when I was getting to know my case manager we talked about what she called my sentence plan, which was all the things we were going to do. I didn't really think it would happen but I thought it all looked like a good idea. Over time I started going to see the basic skills tutor, I joined the group for drug users and then later to learn about anger management. Every so often I saw my case manager and she always seemed to know how I was getting on. I always felt she was interested in me and really cared if I was doing well and that made me want to try harder.'

Introduction

The previous chapters have described several strategies to use when undertaking pro-social work with clients (and colleagues). These are: being a pro-social role model; assertiveness and assertive pro-social feedback; helping the client to develop their motivation; and coaching and supporting the client through behaviour change. These can all be used separately or together in one-off encounters and in longer-term, professional relationships. But how do you systematise a longer period of pro-social work, especially bearing in mind that your client may be at best reluctant and at worst downright unwilling?

A continuing, productive professional relationship requires the worker to be constantly aware of their importance as a pro-social role model and to be looking out for opportunities to reinforce their client's pro-social behaviour and expressions. Fortunately working pro-socially only requires us to model coping, not excellence, so if the worker slips from their desired pro-social behaviour this will give them an opportunity to model other pro-social behaviour such as apologising and/or putting mistakes right.

This chapter looks at further ways of engaging the client as a partner in their own change process in such a way that change can be sustained and consolidated over a period of time, while encouraging the client towards a more pro-social lifestyle.

An integrated approach

Using his own and other people's research Trotter (1999) identifies that an integrated approach to work with the involuntary client requires the following:

- **Accurate role clarification**: We have already seen how the client and the worker can both be socialised into their respective roles, and a warm, empathetic professional relationship, with appropriate boundaries, can be established.

- **Reinforcing and modelling pro-social values**: In order to do this we have to be clear what these values are, how we are going to transmit these to the client both formally in the rules and sanctions set down for our particular project and less formally in the many behaviours and pro-social expressions that we encourage.

- **Collaborative problem solving**: This means a systematic approach to problem solving which incorporates the client's own assessment of the problems, the relative importance of the problems and a range of achievable strategies to tackle them.

Systematic, collaborative problem solving involves answering the following three questions (adapted from Trotter 1999):

1   **What** problems does the client have?
2   **Which** of these are we* going to deal with and in what order?
3   **How** are we* going to deal with the problems?

(*The 'we' in this case is the client, the worker, and possibly others such as the family, partners and/or workers in partner organisations, all or some of whom may be working in collaboration.)

Within these questions is another set of questions that relate to roles and goals:

- **What are our goals**, what are we trying to achieve, what is the big picture here?
- **Who is going to do what?** What is the contract between client and worker?

These are the questions that the worker needs to be asking him or herself to check that the work with the client has some kind of focus and is not just aimless. These questions do not have to be verbalised and they do not necessarily have to come in any particular order. Clients' lives and clients' problems do not usually develop or resolve in a neat logical way. The client's and the worker's view of what the problem is, or what the most important problem is, might change over time. Although it is logical to have a sense of what problems the client has before asking which are we going to deal with or how are we going to deal with them, it is important to return to the whole set of questions every so often.

What problems does the client have?

Studious readers of this book will see a problem in this question. I have been consistently advocating working in a solution-focused way and now I am suggesting looking at problems. I am not suggesting that you ask the client 'what problems do you have?' It is possible to find out about problems by using solution-focused questions such as:

- What would you like to be different?
- How will you know that things are better?
- What changes would make an improvement in things?
- If you were to wake up one morning and everything was all right what would be different? (This is the ultimate 'miracle question' and runs the risk of prompting so big an answer that you would not know where to start.)

Other solution-focused language to use with the client might include referring to problems as 'things they would like to change' or 'issues' for them. It may be easier and more motivating for clients to feel they are working towards possible solutions than to eliminate problems. For instance, it sounds much more motivating to talk about 'helping someone to improve their reading and writing', than 'helping them to solve their literacy problems'.

You and the client may not agree what the problem is, or what needs to change to make a difference to their life. Assessment systems (see discussion of OASys in the story below) may lead to factors being included in treatment/sentence plans that the client does not 'buy into'. It is easy for us to see clients as agents of their own misfortune when they might see themselves as victims of circumstances beyond their control; often the reality is somewhere between the two.

Michael was a fast and rather inconsiderate driver; he drove around in an old banger, vibrating with loud music. He was stopped by the police several times over a short period and became convinced that he was the victim of a racist vendetta. There was probably an element of racism in the fact that he was stopped so many times: he was very visible as a black man in a noisy car. However, there was probably also some legitimate concern that his driving was dangerous and his car might not be roadworthy.

Michael become more and more angry at being stopped so many times by the police; they had never actually prosecuted him for anything and had only warned him about his driving or the state of his car. Matters finally came to a head when he was stopped yet again. He leapt out of the car and started yelling at the police officer and things rapidly got out of control. Michael ended up hitting the police officer and being prosecuted for assault. The police officer said that he had stopped Michael because neither of his brake lights was working and this was shown to be true.

Michael was very lucky he did not get sent to prison but he did get sentenced to a Community Order.

As part of his CO his offender manager (a probation worker) tried to get him to address his offending behaviour. The issue was, what was the cause of the offending behaviour?

Michael still felt strongly that he had been mistreated by the police, to a point that he could not reasonably be expected to tolerate. Even though he accepted that there was a problem with his car, he felt he had only reacted the way he did because he was a victim of police racism.

Jamail, his offender manager who had experienced a good deal of racism himself, had a certain amount of sympathy with Michael's point of view. However, he took the view that Michael had no control over whether the police stopped him, apart possibly from buying a less noticeable car, or indeed whether the police were racist. Taking a cognitive behavioural perspective (see Chapter 1), Jamail believed that, however much Michael **felt and thought** that he was the victim in the situation, he could learn to **behave** differently, that is more calmly, so that if he was stopped again the situation was less likely to get out of hand. Jamail also had a professional obligation to put over several pro-social messages including 'it is wrong to hit people including police officers' and 'it is wrong to drive around in a car that is not roadworthy'. Jamail thought that the most helpful thing he could do was to work with Michael on anger management. This was also an appropriate thing for Jamail to do in his role as a probation service employee as it was the thing that was most likely to reduce the risk of Michael reoffending. However, he could see that this would have no impact unless he could help Michael move from seeing himself as a victim of circumstances to a person who had a problem (lack of control) that could be addressed. He needed to do all this without denying or trivialising the reality of Michael's experience of racism.

In order for Jamail to engage successfully with Michael in the problem solving process he had to develop a good working relationship. He had to be able to empathise with Michael to the extent that he could ask questions and make statements that challenged Michael's perceptions while still keeping a level of trust and rapport between them. He had to use motivational skills and techniques such as those described in Chapter 5. He had to listen to Michael and acknowledge how powerfully Michael believed in his perception of the problem, without colluding with it.

To complicate matters even more, some problem analysis had already taken place in the form of OASys (Offender Assessment System, NPD 2002). In common with many other agencies the offender management services (probation and prison) have an assessment system. At the pre-sentence report stage the interviewing officer fills in a multiple question form answering both factual and subjective questions on the offender. This form is used to assess the offender's risk of reoffending and the risk of harm to themselves and others. This in turn will inform the 'sentence plan'. In Michael's case the sentence plan identified anger management as one priority. Michael might even go along with it to get through his order but nevertheless if he did not come round to thinking that this was really a problem for him, he was unlikely to engage with any work undertaken with him.

Over a period of time a good working relationship grew between the two men and Michael admitted to Jamail that he had problems in other areas of his life because he found it difficult to control his temper, and they began to work on anger management. Michael also began to see that even when he was the victim of racism he had some choices about how to respond. On his way home from a meeting at the probation office Michael was stopped by the police again. By a huge effort of will he managed to be polite to the policeman who stopped him. The officer warned him that he should be wearing his seat belt and to Michael's astonishment let him go on his way.

Trotter (2004) suggests that sometimes client and worker may be able to agree to work on the problem that the worker thinks is most important and the one the client thinks is most important even if these are two different things. This would not work in the above case where the only thing that was within Michael's control was to change his own behaviour; he could only change the behaviour of the police indirectly by the way that he himself behaved.

Making the problem manageable

It may be necessary at this stage to break down the problem into something manageable to work with. For instance, a client says she cannot cope. Does this mean she cannot cope with practical things like getting the children off to school in the morning, or living on a very restricted income, or does she mean she cannot cope because she is depressed or mentally ill? Alternatively, talking in solution-focused terms does this mean she wants to get better at organising the children, managing on a small income (or finding a way of increasing her income) or feeling better herself?

Also it may be necessary to help the client translate the problem (or solution) into something tangible that they can work on and they can see themselves to be working on. In the example above, not being able to cope is intangible and non-specific but if it is broken down into its practical manifestations then it is much easier to see something tangible to work on. Similarly if clients talk about feeling guilty or being worried it is helpful with to work out with them how these feelings manifest themselves as behaviour in their everyday life. Often they can then work towards changing behaviours that will in turn make them feel better.

> Julie had three young children and sought help because she felt unable to cope. She had a warm and loving relationship with the children but was hopelessly disorganised to the point that the family ran out of food and clean clothes and the children were always late for school. Her support worker helped her to see that she was well able to cope with making the children feel loved, secure and happy which were all fundamentally important. With regard to the organisation Julie and her support worker made a step by step plan to help her organise herself. They started with shopping for food and planning meals and when Julie felt a bit more confident about that they moved onto getting the children to school on time. The worker also helped Julie to recognise that she had a huge amount to cope with and encouraged her to enlist more help from her partner.

In Michael's case his original perception of the problem was that it was inevitable that he would get into trouble because his behaviour was the result of the police's behaviour. Jamail helped him to see that although he felt victimised this did not inevitably mean he had to behave in a particular way. Jamail also helped him to work on one element of his behaviour: controlling his temper.

What problems are we going to deal with and in what order (sequencing)?

It may well be the case that when we have identified what we need or want to work with we end up with a lengthy shopping list of problems or, using solution-focused language, a list of aspirations for improvement. (The 'we' in this sentence refers to the client and the worker collaborating.) The danger is this seems overwhelming and unachievable so the role of the worker is to help the client to sort out which problems they are going to deal with and in what order.

Various factors come into play when sorting priorities and these are discussed below.

Risk, need and crises
In some cases there may be factors that over-ride all others. For instance, if a client is homeless or in very insecure housing or chaotic substance misuses it is unlikely that they are able to give much attention to other matters. Similarly if they are at risk of harm from someone (e.g. a violent partner), or pose a risk of harm to someone (e.g. a child), or pose a risk to themselves (e.g. are suicidal) the worker must do something about this first.

Organisational constraints
As we have already seen working pro-socially involves working according to the formal and informal rules and values of your organisation as well as of society as whole. Most organisations have an over-riding aim. In the story of Michael and his case manager, probation worker Jamail, the OASys assessment will lead Jamail into prioritising working on criminogenic needs, i.e. those which lead to offending (anger management in Michael's case). There is a fine balance to be struck between the client's and the worker's perception of problems when deciding which problems to work on and in which order. But when working pro-socially the emphasis needs to be on encouraging the client to work with the problems that caused them to be a client in the first place. However, even in the case where there is a clear organisational imperative to prioritise certain issues, the worker still needs to engage the client in the process and to take account of the client's perception of their problems too.

> Tony was working with 'school refusers'. He and his organisation were judged on their ability to get children back into school. By the time children came to his notice they had often been out of school for years. Often the original reason that they had stopped going to school had become obscured by overwhelming fears and anxieties about re-entering an institution where the other children and the learning had moved on without them. Tony had to manage a delicate balance between reinforcing the pro-social message that ultimately they had to get some schooling, and helping them to move on from their fears, many of which were about the very thing he was encouraging them towards.

A problem that is manageable and has a good chance of being resolved
We have already seen that it is helpful to break problems down into small manageable chunks. Problem solving is better with something that is manageable and has a good chance of success. This might be because it has a practical solution that the worker has some control over. However, the client still has to engage with the problem solving process; they have to be motivated to do something about it (see also 'small steps', in Chapter 6).

The client sees the problem as a problem and/or is ready to do something about it
However clearly the worker might see the problem, if the client does not think that there is a problem, or is not motivated to do something about it, then the first priority might be to bring them to a state of readiness.

A probation worker may have the facility to refer clients both to literacy classes and employment preparation groups; however, if the client does not see literacy and/or unemployment as the problem(s) or is not ready to do anything about it this is likely to have little or no impact. This might indicate the need for motivational work with the client before or alongside referral.

Pro-social values
Sometimes the client might want to work on problems and goals in a way that is not consistent with pro-social values and the worker will need to discourage this.

> A tenant support officer was working with a group of tenants in a small cul-de-sac. They had fallen out over issues such as noisy children, dogs getting into gardens and the fact that one tenant was running a small-scale car repair and sales business from his house. The tenant support worker was acting as a mediator; he was

encouraging the group to sort out which issues were negotiable and to work together on these. He had to be quite clear with the man who was running the car business that this was illegal and had to stop and there was no question of using mediation to encourage the neighbours to be more tolerant of the business.

What are our goals, what are we trying to achieve: what is the big picture?

Goals are the incentive, the motive for change that will keep both the worker and the client on track. Both Trotter (1999) and O'Connell (1998) refer to a considerable body of research that indicates having clear, simple and attainable goals improves the prospect of a satisfactory outcome for problem solving. O'Connell also suggests that the chances of a satisfactory outcome are improved if the goals are defined positively.

Goals should be written down so that they can be referred back to and should be simple and specific so there is no room for disagreement about their meaning.

It is often suggested that goals should be SMART, that is:

- **Specific**: Written in such a way that there is no confusion about what they describe.

- **Measurable**: Written in such a way that within the description is some way of knowing whether it has been achieved or not.

- **Achievable**: The goal needs to be something that the client can realistically aspire to, so often goals need to be broken down into incremental chunks.

- **Realistic or relevant**: The goal needs to be something that the client sees as important (see earlier comments on motivation and engaging the client) and as taking them nearer to their eventual bigger goals.

- **Time-bounded**: There needs to be a time limit built in or a review time in order to encourage the client and worker to look back at intervals and see how they are progressing.

What is the contract between client and worker (who is going to do what)?

The contracting process, both formal and informal, between client and worker starts from the first contact. Establishing role boundaries and ground rules as discussed in Chapter 3 is part of the contract even if it is not formally written down. However, as part of collaborative problem solving both what is to be done and who is to do it needs to be formalised. Ideally this should be in the form of a written contract agreed by both parties. In practice this depends on the context in which the work takes place. It would seem appropriate and in fact desirable for a client and worker to have a written contract in a setting such as probation or other offender supervision. In a setting such as a youth club, a youth worker and a young person may be working towards an agreed goal and agree who is going to do what but it may not feel appropriate to write this down.

How are we going to deal with problems?

The next stage in problem solving is to identify the methods and strategies for achieving the goals identified.

Solutions may be generated or at least initiated by worker and client working together. For instance, you might use the model described in Chapter 6 to help the client develop the skills and confidence to deal with a challenging situation. Or together you might work out a strategy for dealing with a difficult situation such as managing a testing teenage son or daughter.

Worker and client may agree tasks for the client to undertake between sessions and report back on next time they meet: for instance, the client may agree to try out in real situations, skills practised using the coaching model in Chapter 6 or to gather some information prior to a further step.

The worker may agree to undertake tasks on behalf of the client such as acting as an advocate (for instance, in getting fine payments rescheduled by the court).

Case management, working with partner agencies

Frequently the worker is not the only person working with the client. He or she may refer them to other parts of the organisation or to other agencies in order to provide specialist or specific solutions. For instance, the correctional services often use a model where an 'offender manager' (case manager) acts as the broker for a range of interventions for an offender. Examples might include in-house intervention such as offending behaviour groups, or hostels and/or external provision from partner organisations such as literacy classes or drug counselling services. The case manager may have a significant face-to-face working relationship with the client, but in some cases (perhaps due to geographical distance or caseloads and priorities) they will have a very limited face-to-face relationship with the client. Another example might be working with a young person who is having some difficulties at school. The key worker might be an educational mentor but they will also be working with teachers and possibly learning support workers and or social workers.

The offender manager or case manager has a responsibility to make the process of referral and the ongoing work with the client consistent with the aims of collaborative, pro-social problem solving. This means ensuring that as far as possible the client is engaged with the reasons for the referral and takes responsibility for such things as getting themselves there.

It also means ensuring the work of the staff at the target agency is consistent with pro-social principles and (with appropriate regard to confidentiality) the staff there have an understanding of the work the primary agency is undertaking. Also that the practice of the agency is consistent with the principles of effective practice – that is, what is known to work and has been shown to work by research. This is likely to be less of an issue where the agency has ongoing partnership arrangements with the primary agency. However, particular care needs to be taken when the agency being referred to is not known so well.

Using the example above of the young person having difficulties at school, encouraging them to join a youth club might help them to increase their confidence and broaden their social circle. But if it turns out that the youth club is very loosely supervised and the child is vulnerable either to bullying or to negative peer group influence, this might not prove to be a very helpful referral.

Most important of all, the client needs to understand the process of referral, who they are going to see and why. The case manager is likely to be the person who helps the client to make sense of the whole process and to integrate the learning from the different interventions.

An effective feedback mechanism should also be in place so that each partner can reinforce and support the work of the other. The limits of confidentiality need to be clear to all parties especially the client.

Sequencing of interventions is particularly important in case management as this can prepare the client for the next intervention. For example, an offender might not be ready to attend a group looking at offending behaviour until their drug use has stabilised and before they have undertaken some motivational work. In the real world of targets and other pressures, sequencing may not be ideal but nevertheless it needs to be taken into account.

A case management arrangement can work very well bringing a range of expertise and solutions to a client; however, the evidence offered throughout this book suggests that positive outcomes are more likely to occur when the primary relationship with the case manager is strong and is maintained throughout the process.

Keeping track, ongoing review

As discussed at the start of this chapter the different elements of collaborative, pro-social problem solving do not necessarily happen in a neat sequence. It may be necessary to return to the key questions again and again as during the life of the working relationship the picture may change considerably. Sometimes changes which are in themselves positive can have wide reaching consequences some of which are negative at least in the short term and which in turn need strategies to deal with them.

> Grace got married when she fell pregnant at the age of 16. Twelve years and four children later, she was bored with her marriage, her husband had no job and she was struggling with a series of low-paid jobs to keep the family together and to look after the children and the house. She was also frustrated with the fact that she had very limited education even though she was quite bright. An offence of deception against a mail order catalogue company brought her to the attention of the probation service. She was lucky as she and her offender manager really hit it off and the offender manager worked with her to boost her confidence. Within weeks she had joined an evening class and shortly afterwards she got a better job. Within six months she had left her husband, but that generated a whole new set of challenges about accommodation, about childcare and about helping the children come to terms with the split.

It is very important that as well as reviewing and reassessing the work still to be done, the worker and client review the road already travelled. It is easy to lose sight of progress already achieved when faced with a seemingly endless new set of problems. This is an opportunity for the worker to do some pro-social reinforcement (rewarding) and to help the client feel empowered by recognising what has been achieved so far.

Summary

The aim of pro-social work is to help people to change. This change process needs to be systematised so that both the worker and the client have a sense of progress made and progress needed. The steps need to be broken down and made manageable and there must be clarity about who is doing what between the worker(s) and the client.

The worker and client need to arrive at a measure of agreement about what problems they are going to be working on. This may take some time and depend on developing rapport and also on motivational work. If the client does not see the problem (or as their problem) they are unlikely to engage successfully in working on it.

The problem should be manageable and may need to be broken down into a series of steps.

The problem solving process needs to be sequenced, that is to have a logical order.

The client and worker must agree what goals they are aiming towards.

The client, the worker and other parties such as the family, partnership agencies, etc. need to agree on who is doing what, in other words, what the contract is.

Everyone involved has understand what is going to be done to tackle the problems, including partner agencies.

The work needs to be reviewed regularly to ensure that progress is being made and that the bigger picture has not changed over time.

8. Responding to individual need and diversity

'I wasn't very happy in my last team, I never really felt included. Nothing I can put my finger on but little things like they never got my name quite right, they always looked a bit uncomfortable when they talked about black people as if they were afraid of saying the wrong thing. The team I am in now are a funny lot in some ways: on the face of it I wouldn't expect to have much in common with them, but they are all genuinely warm and friendly. If they don't know something about me or my culture they ask, they are sensitive to things that I might find embarrassing (like going down the pub) so they check things out with me. My manager sets the tone. He said on day one that he expects his team to value and embrace diversity and they do. I've never known a gay man before but he is so openly 'out' that I've learned loads from him and strangely I have found that our experiences of discrimination give us some shared perspectives.'

Introduction

In order to work pro-socially we need to make every effort to understand and value other people's perspective and experience and not to make assumptions about them. There are as many diversity issues as there are people and we do not need to be experts in specific issues. What is much more important is to be prepared to engage actively in developing and modelling our own anti-discriminatory practice. We need to be sensitive to difference and to resist the temptation to assume that we are the norm. We need to accept that we will ourselves have prejudices. We need to be prepared to challenge and to be challenged, to take risks and to be willing to learn.

If we ignore diversity we perpetuate discrimination. Tuklo Associates (1999) developed a model they called the 'Cycle of Complacency' to assist hostel staff to explore their work with residents from ethnic minorities. An absence of provision for ethnic minorities means that there are likely to be fewer referrals. The few people who do get referred are likely to have poorer outcomes because of the lack of provision. The poor track record with these clients leads to a disinclination to refer. This leads in turn to the perception by staff that the service is not needed because they do not have many ethnic minority clients anyway.

This model is equally applicable to other work settings and/or other diversity issues. It reminds us that in order to make our service truly accessible to a diverse client group we have to ensure that we are going out of our way to identify and address their needs.

Issues of responsiveness and diversity are such a fundamental part of pro-social practice that they run throughout the book. However, they deserve a chapter (or possibly a book) in their own right and because of this it was difficult to decide what to put in and what to leave out. In making the final decision about the chapter I have tried to bear in mind what the busy but reflective practitioner would find useful and thought provoking, but this is not to say that other topics in this area are not important.

One size definitely does not fit all

The causes of offending and other anti-social behaviour and the factors that change that behaviour are multi-factorial and complex. There is relatively little research that addresses specific groups other than white male working-class offenders (Kemshall *et al.* 2004a; Chigwada-Bailey 2003). We do not have a great deal of evidence, for instance, that tells us whether the path into and out of offending is different for people from minority ethnic groups as opposed to white people. We know more about women's offending but little about the differences between women from different ethnic groups (Chigwada-Bailey 2003). We do not know a great deal about the link between offending and mental heath problems or literacy difficulties. Limited research and common sense tell us that some paths into and out of anti-social behaviour are likely to be similar, but others are likely to be specific to those groups and/or specifically related to being a member of that group.

It is easy to see the clients we work with as members of groups that share the same attributes: sex offenders, teenage parents, black youths, etc. Often projects are set up for such specific groups and appropriately provide help with problems and issues that they have in common. Yet every one of those people is at the centre of their own world and you can be pretty certain that although they have things in common, they will also see themselves as different and unique in relation to the other people in the group.

A lot of the current work with offenders is underpinned by the belief that their offending behaviour can be changed by helping the offender to understand how their thinking and feeling affects the way they behave (see section in Chapter 1 on cognitive behavioural theory, also McGuire, 2000). This then allows the offender to exercise more appropriate choices about the way in which they behave and thus behave more pro-socially. Much of this book is about helping people to behave differently by showing and teaching new behaviours. However, many offenders and other people who behave anti-socially would see their behaviour as a response to something that has happened to them and in many cases we might agree with them. For example, among the offender population there is a disproportionate number of people with literacy difficulties (Davies *et al.* 2004). They may (and we may) see their offending as a response to the fact that other opportunities to gain income lawfully are limited if they cannot read or write and that their inability to read and write is due to failures in their schooling.

There is also a disproportionate number of black people in the offender population (Hollis *et al.* 2003). The reasons for this are many and complex, including racism inherent in the criminal justice system (Hearnden and Hough 2004), but it is likely that some black offenders see their offending as a response to the alienation they feel from the society within which they live. While we may not condone the offending or other anti-social behaviour we may have considerable sympathy with the feelings of alienation or rejection.

When trying to work pro-socially the challenge is, on the one hand, to balance the need to encourage people to choose to conform more closely to what is considered to be appropriate (pro-social) behaviour, while on the other hand taking account of the perspective and the needs of the individual. It is also to provide a core service of an appropriate standard to everyone, while acknowledging that some people need more or different services and thus avoiding a 'one size fits all' approach.

Diversity is about similarity and difference and is about all of us

It is easy to start thinking diversity is a problem and that trying to work in a diverse way is to run the risk of falling into traps set to catch you. It is easy to see diversity as being about people who are different from the norm, but the same as all others with the same attributes. The norm is often seen as being white, heterosexual, able-bodied, middle class and probably male. In fact, in any group of people there will be things that they all have in common, things that some have in common with a few people in the group and things that are unique about each individual. The similarities between people are often the way into accepting and understanding the differences.

> The three black members of a team of seven felt that they were being unfairly treated by their white manager and that this was due to the manager's inexperience with managing black people. However, in conversation with their colleagues who were all white they discovered that they were also experiencing problems with the manager. Over time, the situation improved, although this required some courageous and assertive feedback from all the staff, and some training and development for the manager. The root of the problem was the manager's lack of experience; this was compounded in her relationship with the black staff by her acute anxiety about 'getting things wrong' with the black team members and her lack of opportunities for training and development around diversity issues.

Diversity then is an **issue** that needs to be addressed but acknowledging and trying to address diversity is **not a problem** but something that enriches relationships.

Looking at diversity from the inside out

Developing anti-discriminatory practice has been described as being like peeling an onion. You take off a layer and your eyes water; just when your eyes stop watering there is another layer to be peeled off and your eyes start to water again.

We all see the world through a filter of our pre-conceptions developed through our experience and our upbringing. As Covey (1999: 28) puts it:

> We see the world not as it is but as we are, or as we are conditioned to see it. When we open our mouths to describe what we see, we in effect describe ourselves, our perceptions and our paradigms.

There is no absolute understanding of diversity issues: our personal thinking and wider thinking and understanding is always changing. As Covey (1999: 29) continues:

> The more we are aware of our basic paradigms, maps, or assumptions, and the extent to which we have been influenced by our experience, the more we can take responsibility for those paradigms, examine them, test them against reality, listen to others and be open to their

perceptions, thereby getting a larger picture and a far more objective view.

In other words we need to engage actively in 'peeling our own onion'. We need to try and be aware of the preconceptions, stereotypes and prejudices that we have internalised and to be ready to take risks and to learn from our mistakes. This can be uncomfortable but the only alternative is to operate in a 'colour blind' way, pretending that differences do not exist. This might make life easier but it makes it impossible to get to know the whole person.

I was recently talking to an Asian woman who told me she was fasting but because she was diabetic she had some emergency food in case she felt ill. This conversation took place in the middle of Ramadan, so I asked her if it was difficult working through Ramadan, to which she replied that she was not Muslim but Hindu. I apologised for having made an assumption and she was very gracious, and I do not think she was particularly offended, but I felt cross with myself.

It was subsequently suggested to me that this was an error that many white people would make and I should not be too hard on myself. It is true that it was an easy mistake to make but only because I was seeing a stereotype of Asian people. I had added up Asian and fasting and come up with Ramadan, without stopping to question myself. I learned something from that experience and I will never make that particular mistake again.

It is important not only to take individual responsibility for challenging our own internalised thinking but also to try and keep up with wider changes in thinking and understanding. This is formally symbolised in changing legislation. Equal opportunities legislation demonstrates a political intention to increase inclusivity and to oppose discrimination. The legislation is updated as thinking moves on. It is also supported by guidance such as the Commission for Racial Equality's Codes of Practice.

Who defines pro-social?

Someone commented that a group work programme I had written for offenders (Cherry 2004a) operated from a white euro-centric perspective. He was right in one sense: it does because it is designed to help offenders problem solve in order to live more pro-social lives and specifically to stop committing offences. Gelsthorpe (2001) discusses arguments to support the idea that both criminological knowledge and criminal justice practices are imbued with white western concepts. What is defined as a criminal offence (and therefore not pro-social) is decided in this British society, which is a white dominated society. The person making the comment had not read the programme at the time, and when he did I hoped he would see that it was designed to convey the message to all participants that the programme was for them. For example, it takes account of varying levels of literacy and learning abilities and learning styles; it avoids stereotypes of the family; it uses visual images of black and white, men and women; group workers are given specific guidance on anti-discriminatory practice, etc.

Gelsthorpe (1998, 2001: 152) poses some questions about pro-social modelling. She was writing with particular reference to Community Service (now Community Punishment or unpaid work) in the probation service; however, I think these are equally applicable to pro-social practice in a broader context.

- What sort of cultural values are being expressed in 'positive role modelling' and whose values are they? How can pro-social and anti-social behaviour be characterised and in what ways, if any, do these characterisations reflect cultural, social or gender differences?

- What social differences are relevant to the discussion? Social differences are endless and not just the obvious ones.

- Is pro-social modelling gendered? Are the values inherent in pro-social modelling closer to feminine ways of thinking and speaking in that they involve forming empathetic relationships? Is it harder or easier for men or women to do pro-social modelling? Is it harder or easier for clients and practitioner to be the same or opposite genders?

- What about notions of legitimate authority? Are there different cultural, class, male or female or other perceptions of authority? Do people of different ages have different perceptions of legitimate authority?

- How can practitioners avoid making assumptions about people's values and understanding of probation practice?

- How can wide social differences in values and different characteristics of offender and practitioner be resolved to the extent that shared language and understanding of the purpose of the focused work can be achieved?

- How can social differences be accommodated in pro-social modelling; how can practitioners ensure that they are able to 'hear' across social differences?

There are no straightforward answers to these questions but as Gelsthorpe (1998, 2001) says they add up to a need for a 'reflexive' (or reflective) practice where the practitioner is conscious of what he or she is bringing to the relationship and how the client might hear what is being said. In other words what micro-messages might be transmitted and how these might be heard. Reflective practice also involves avoiding treating clients as a homogenous group and taking the time to get to know them as individuals. It means recognising not only when anti-social behaviour is a response to cultural or gender issues as described above, but also when response to the client–worker relationship may be a gender or culturally mediated behaviour.

> Junior was a young black offender sentenced to Community Punishment after being involved in a gang fight. In his one-to-one interactions with his CP supervisor, a white man, he was cooperative, friendly and keen to engage. He showed genuine remorse, expressed a desire to break away from his peers in the gang, and was keen to undertake training and qualifications. In his first work party he was placed with some young black men from his home area. As far as the supervisor was concerned, in this group he was a pain in the neck, rude, loud and uncooperative. He also kept talking to his friends in patois, which meant that the supervisor did not know what they were talking about. His supervisor quickly realised that the peer group pressure was so great that it was unreasonable to expect Junior to be seen to be being cooperative with a white man in front of several of his friends. He moved him to another work party where he was not with anyone he knew and Junior's behaviour was no problem at all.

When thinking about who defines pro-social it is also useful to bear in mind who defines racist or any other discriminatory behaviour. Macpherson (1999), in the inquiry into the murder of Stephen Lawrence, stated that the police should take the widest possible interpretation of racially motivated crime, and if the victim believed the behaviour to be racist it should be defined as racist. This is widely described as the Macpherson definition of racism but it can also be applied to other discriminatory behaviour such as sexism, homophobia, etc.

So far this chapter has probably offered more questions than answers. However, this is in the nature of peeling the onion of anti-discriminatory practice. There are so many factors to take into account that the reflective pro-social practitioner must ask themselves questions all the time.

Managing the micro-messages

Micro-messages are the small messages, often unintentional and often unnoticed by the sender, which we constantly send and receive. Micro-messages can have a powerful effect on our interactions with others. Micro in this context means small, not unimportant. Individually micro-messages are by their nature small and ephemeral; they may be hard to identify let alone challenge. Negative micro-messages can be described as micro-inequities (Rose 1999) which can lead to mistrust in the recipient, damage self-esteem and reduce the possibility of developing a constructive relationship. Examples of micro-inequities are: failing to take the trouble to learn a name which is unfamiliar in one's own culture or language; failing to recognise a person of a different race because 'they all look the same'; assuming that someone's partner is of the opposite sex to themselves; only having images of white people in publicity material or posters. When I was in my first management job, people frequently assumed that my male deputy was the senior manager. Their first interaction would be addressed to him and then when I introduced myself, or he diverted them to me, there would be an almost imperceptible missed beat as they readjusted their perception. As a young woman, struggling with my confidence in a very challenging job, the repeated message that it was unexpected to find me in a manager's role did nothing to help.

People who belong to groups that have been historically discriminated against sometimes find themselves hypersensitive to micro-inequities. People who belong to the dominant group will probably find it hard to see many of the micro-messages they are sending because they start, consciously or unconsciously, from the view that where they stand is the norm.

In the interests of anti-discriminatory practice we need to try to manage the micro-messages so that we minimise micro-inequities and maximise positive micro-messages. Sometimes this requires a self-conscious effort and may seem contrived but nevertheless it is very important. In many service venues (schools, hospitals, probation offices, prisons, etc.) you will see posters that have images of people of many races, both genders and sometimes with obvious disabilities as well as posters or notices which explicitly make statements about diversity. These are attempts to give a fairly subtle, positive message about the service being an inclusive service.

Awareness raising, training, constructive feedback, self-questioning are all ways to develop awareness and to manage the micro-messages. Mentoring, coaching personal development and skills development are ways in which the recipients of micro-inequities can be helped to deal with them and lessen their effects. Positive role models from members of the same group as themselves can be particularly helpful. For instance, a gay member of staff who is confidently 'out' in the work setting makes it much easier for gay clients to also be 'out' and to feel confident they are less likely to experience homophobia in that setting.

The language we use to describe people

The terms that we use can be very important in symbolising our attitude to discrimination and inclusivity. For instance, there is a difference in attitude implied between the terms 'disabled person' and 'person with disabilities'. The latter implies that the disability is only part of the whole person and the former implies that the whole person is being described in terms of their disability. Even more inclusive is the term 'person with different abilities' or 'differently abled person' which implies that the person in question is not being judged against a norm of able-bodied people but is simply different, not lacking in some way.

The terms used to describe people from ethnic minority communities are full of meaning. This group is sometimes collectively described as black. 'Black' is not a literal but political description reflecting the common experience of people of colour as opposed to white people. Sometimes on courses (white) people tell me they feel uncomfortable using the term 'black' because they feel it is derogatory in some way and they have been brought up to use the term 'coloured'. My understanding of the term 'coloured' is that is was used in apartheid South Africa in a pejorative way to describe people of mixed white and black parentage and is therefore an offensive term to most black people. However, the term 'people of colour' is sometimes used, particularly in the USA. The term 'black' is increasingly coming to be understood to refer to people of African-Caribbean origin (not Afro-Caribbean, afro is a hair cut). The term 'black and minority ethnic' (BME) is sometimes used as a more all-encompassing term for the collective group of people of colour. I have studiously avoided using the term 'non-whites' in this paragraph, and indeed in this book, because that term implies that to be white is the norm. 'Nigger' is a term that has deeply offensive associations with slavery and with holding black people in contempt. However, I believe that within some groups of black people the term has been reclaimed and is widely used, although I also know other black people find this unacceptable and I cannot imagine any circumstances where it would be an appropriate term for a white person to use.

Increasingly people referred to as Asians are rejecting that label in favour of a religious identity (Manzoor 2005). Manzoor says the term Asian was developed in the 1940s by colonial administrators to describe the citizens of the newly independent India and Pakistan. In the 1970s it gained currency among 'Asians' themselves as a way of distinguishing themselves from the larger group identified as 'black'. However, the term 'Asian' ignores the differences in religion, experience and expectations among the people who originate from the Indian sub-continent. Also the use of the term to describe such a disparate group identifies them in terms of what they are **not** (not white or black) rather than what they individually **are** (Sikh, Muslim, Hindu, Christian, etc.).

As I write this I know someone is going to read it and wince, but I am trying to demonstrate how powerful language is and how, as part of peeling our personal onion, we have to try and understand the subtle nuances of meaning and how this changes over time.

Challenging discriminatory behaviour and attitudes

We know from research (Trotter 1999) that if we do not challenge anti-social behaviours and expressions we can be seen to be condoning them or even colluding with them. So when working with clients who demonstrate discriminatory attitudes and behaviour, either related to the reason they have become a client (racially motivated offenders, for instance) or as part of the supervisory relationship, we need to find ways of challenging them. This is often easier to say than do, but it is the responsibility of all of us, not just the people who are seen to be the direct targets of the discrimination.

Blatantly discriminatory statements ('gays should not be allowed to bring up children', 'all Rastafarians are drug-taking, lazy people', 'all Muslims are potential terrorists', all of which I have heard recently) are often hard to challenge but must be challenged. It is often more difficult to know whether to challenge more subtle statements and behaviours especially as they often come from well-intentioned but naive people: for instance, the person who in passing refers to all managers as 'he', or the prison officer who refers to prisoners as 'cons' or the person who describes someone in a wheelchair as 'handicapped'. However, it is important to remember that if you do not challenge the person they are unlikely to ever change, and if they are genuinely well-meaning they will listen and change. Also if you do not challenge the behaviour you are implicitly condoning it.

The tools that are described in this book for changing behaviour are equally applicable to challenging discriminatory behaviours and attitudes. Motivational techniques can be used for encouraging people to think about what they are saying and to explore the inconsistencies in what they say. Pro-social feedback can be used to challenge clients' or colleagues' behaviour while still demonstrating regard for the whole person. Assertiveness is useful to articulate your own position very clearly without getting into an argument with the client. Some deeply entrenched behaviours and attitudes are very difficult to challenge and you may need specialist help and support (see, for example, *From Murmur to Murder* (Kay and Gast 1998) or *www.raceaction.net*). A recent report (Bridges 2005) states that in most cases probation officers fail to challenge the attitudes and behaviour of convicted racists and sometimes explain away their racism as drunkenness or out of character.

There are as many diversity issues as there are people and I have highlighted general points which apply to many individuals and groups of people; however, the rest of this chapter highlights some issues for specific groups which the pro-social practitioner needs to think about. This is in no way an exhaustive list.

Identity: colour, race, ethnic origin, ethnicity, religion

Increasing understanding of people's sense of their own identity is important when working pro-socially because it reduces the risk that we will make incorrect assumptions about them. It also allows us to engage more with the 'real' person – the person the client sees themselves to be. This understanding is not only important in developing our own anti-discriminatory practice: it is also helpful when challenging discrimination by clients. One aspect of anti-social behaviour is racism and understanding the focus of racist behaviour in the individual (e.g. is it aimed primarily at colour, ethnicity or religion?) gives us a better chance of tackling this.

Colour
Usually the term 'colour' is used to distinguish between white and black people. It is political rather than literal in its meaning and is an important distinction because people are often treated differently simply because they do not share the skin colour of the majority population. However, this does not mean that everyone of the same or similar skin colour necessarily has other things in common.

Race
This is harder to define as it is used in different ways. It is often used to describe people who originate from the same part of the world, which begs the question if people who come from the same part of the world have common experiences. (For instance, would a Muslim from Pakistan see themselves as having more in common with a non-Muslim from Pakistan or a Muslim from India, the Middle East or Britain?) The term 'mixed race' is often used to describe children who have parents who

originate from different parts of the world and particularly when the parents have different skin colour. This is sometimes seen as a pejorative term and 'dual heritage' can be used as an alternative term. In certain contexts race can have very negative connotations, for instance, in phrases such as 'purity of the race' used by the Nazis and similar groups.

Ethnic origin

This is a term used officially to describe groups of people who originate in the same part of the world. For example, the CRE's (2004) self-definition categories are:

- White British
- White Irish
- Other white
- Asian or Asian British–Indian
- Asian or Asian British–Pakistani
- Asian or Asian British–Bangladeshi
- Asian or Asian British–Other
- Black or Black British–Caribbean
- Black or Black British–African
- Black or Black British–other
- Chinese or other ethnic group–Chinese
- Chinese or other ethnic group–other

A 'mixed' category is also sometimes offered.

Ethnicity

Ethnicity is often used by people to identify those that they feel they have most in common with due to a mixture of genetics, history and experience. For instance, an Iraqi Kurd placed in an asylum seekers' hotel with other Iraqis would possibly see the most important factor of their identity not as their race (Iraqi?) or colour (black or non-white?) or their ethnic origin ('Chinese or other ethnic groups–other' according to the CRE) but as their ethnicity (Kurdish). This would be because their over-riding experiences in Iraq would probably be of persecution because of their Kurdish ethnicity and of support and solidarity with other Kurds.

Religion or faith

This for many people is the most important factor in their identity and it is also the way in which they are most clearly identified by others. For instance, since the events of 9/11 and the subsequent Afghan and Iraq wars, people of Muslim faith living in Britain have been subjected to increasing amounts of discrimination (Ameli *et al.* 2004). The level of discrimination appears, however, to be different depending on the racial origins of the Muslims. The total number of Indian Muslims reporting discrimination was 77%, Pakistani Muslims 82% and white Muslims 88%. The white Muslims appear to have been labelled traitors to their race but we have to remember that the proportion of white people in the sample was very small and the number of non-white Muslims suffering discrimination because of their religion is much greater.

Gender and pro-social practice: issues to think about

Is the anti-social behaviour to do with being a man/woman and should that be a factor in the client/worker interaction?

Much of the research on offending and other deviance has either been concerned with men and boys or has researched a mixed gender population but failed to differentiate factors affecting men and women. There has always been a substrand of criminology that looked at the specific experience of women and at what part of women's offending is to do with being a woman. There is an increasing amount of research that looks at what part of male deviance has to do with being a man; however, with the exception of domestic or sexual violence it has had relatively little impact on practice.

Truly pro-social practice in being responsive to the individual cannot be gender neutral, in other words, it has to take into account the different life experiences of men and women and the impact this has on them. The information that follows relates to criminal behaviour but relates to other anti-social behaviour as well.

Chigwada-Bailey (2003) points out that there is even less specific research on the experience of black women and factors that are to do with being both black and a woman.

Relatively few women commit crimes. Less than 3 per cent of the prison population in 2002 was female (Hollis 2003). In 2002, 17 per cent of the female prison population was black minority ethnic (BME) even though only 8 per cent of the total population is BME. Women have fewer previous convictions and tend to commit less serious offences. Women's offences are predominantly of a less serious nature, often financial. A lot of women's crime is to do directly with being a woman: prostitution, offences to do with cruelty to children, etc. A significant number of women offenders have also been subject to abuse in childhood or domestic violence. There is a rise in drugs related offences among women but these still tend to be at the less serious end of the spectrum.

A research report (Smith 2003) suggests that in early teenage years boys are only slightly likely to be more deviant than girls but by the age of 15, although girls also indulge in some activities such as smoking and drinking, boys are much more likely to be involved in serious offending. The author suggests that there is a risk factor to which males are prone, that is implicated in serious offending but which is not identified by their research. Also perpetrators and the victims are often the same people. They found that violent girls were very different from other girls; they were more likely to be gang members, truants and from a lower-class background. On the other hand violent boys were much like their friends and their behaviour was in some way a 'normal' part of growing up as a boy (2003: 7), particularly within certain social groups. The report begins to identify some of the differences between boys and girls that lead to these findings. For instance, the fact that girls are better able to negotiate their way out of difficulty, and do not 'hang out' in places where violence takes place, in the way boys do.

Does the gender of the worker make a difference?

A situation in which a male is working with a female client runs the risk of replicating a previous oppressive relationship. On the other hand it could open up the possibility to model a different pattern of male behaviour.

A feminist analysis might suggest that a woman working with a female client would open up the possibility for a shared perspective on the experience of being a woman in a male dominated society. On the other hand other differences such as race or class would be more important.

Women workers working with men could be accused of having little understanding of a male perspective. This is becoming an issue in the Probation Service where it is proving much easier to recruit women than men and offenders (mostly male and working class) have an increasing chance of being supervised by women (mostly younger and middle class). The problem does not lie with the individual women but with the lack of an overall gender mix available for supervising.

Workers have the opportunity to model different ways of relating to the opposite sex. It is very important therefore that members of a team demonstrate respect for one another at all times.

Mike worked in a male prison. In his team were two women, one of whom was considered by many people to be stunningly attractive. The male prisoners were always trying to wind him up about how he must fancy her. He was scrupulous in demonstrating respectful behaviour to all his colleagues and in nipping the sexist jokes in the bud. One evening he was chatting to a couple of prisoners. They said they had noticed how he treated her the same as everyone else and asked him 'how he managed to keep his hands off her.' He sensed that this enquiry had a serious element and was not just a ➥

> prurient one and this set off a discussion about the role of women at work and the relationship between men and women. He noticed afterwards that the prisoners were more respectful to his colleague.

Do women or men receive a poorer service when they are in a significant minority within a group?

In many criminal justice settings there are fewer women who may be working in male-oriented jobs. For instance there are 100 Probation Approved Premises (hostels), of these four are women only and 28 are mixed (Foster 2003). In mixed hostels there are usually very few women (typically three or four in a hostel with 22 men). Consequently the services are going to be geared primarily for men. However, the women in mixed hostels have very specific needs (i.e. safety, privacy, etc.). Although mixed hostels are generally considered in the service to be undesirable, if they are phased out it will mean even less choice about the geographical location of women's bed spaces, which could create a new set of problems for the clients. So while such hostels exist, staff need to be acutely sensitive to the particular issues the hostels generate for their women residents.

Some services for parents such as play groups, Sure Start, and parenting groups often predominantly attract women, as they are usually the primary carers. However, there are also men who are primary carers and steps should be taken to ensure that they do not feel excluded in a female dominated environment.

Is treating men and women the same unfair?

The female prison population is rising faster proportionately than the male one. Chigwada-Bailey (2003) suggests that this is because since the 1991 Criminal Justice Act there has been an increasing tendency to sentence according to the offence not the offender. This has meant that an increasing number of women with children, addictions, mental health issues or a history of abuse, are being sent to prison. Is this then perpetuating a cycle that makes their children more vulnerable to deviance because of the separation from their mothers?

Again, more questions than answers. Nevertheless food for thought when understanding the intricacies of the client–worker relationship and the factors that need to be taken into account when helping and encouraging people to change.

Learning and thinking styles

One of the things that is rarely taken into account when thinking about communicating with clients is the way in which they absorb information and learn. There are no right or wrong thinking styles, but as in everything else discussed in this chapter, not everyone is the same and in order to work pro-socially we need to be sensitive to differences. There are various models of thinking and learning styles but the VAK model described below is simple and accessible and in my experience is one which practitioners find really useful.

Bandler and Grinder (1975) identified three thinking modalities, visual, auditory and kinaesthetic. It helps to think of these as the triggers or switches that turn the brain on to learning.

Visual learners
These learners will take in information best through their eyes. In order to make sense of what is being said they will want to see it, in some form. Many people have this preference, which is why so many lecturers, teachers, etc. use visual aids. For many adults learning a new activity – such as using a machine to wash their clothes, or making a phone call – it is far easier to visually understand what is required of them when the coach demonstrates the necessary movements, than just telling them (verbal) what to do.

The language that people use often reflects the way in which they take in information. For instance, the visual learner may use phrases such as 'the way I see it' or 'I picture it as …'. Often visual thinkers will literally draw a picture to describe something.

Auditory learners
Auditory learners will be more satisfied with a verbal description. They are tuned into making sense of the world through what they hear. They are more likely to be good with words, and be able to describe what is expected of them and what they are doing. They will hear what is going on around them, and will be sensitive to extraneous noises, which they will find very distracting. When learning to use the washing machine the auditory learner will probably appreciate a verbal description of what to do. The auditory learner might say something like 'what I heard him say was …' or 'let me tell you the story of what happened'.

Kinaesthetic learners
These learners take in information through their body, both the emotions and the actual muscular activity. The kinaesthetic person learning to

use the washing machine will need to actually have a go themselves. Language that they use might include 'I felt really good' or 'I experienced it as ...'.

The understanding of different ways of taking in information is having a profound effect on education with a move a way from 'chalk and talk' towards more multimodal methods. The significance of this for pro-social practice is that we need to think about the ways in which we communicate with people all the time to ensure that they are actually receiving the message.

The first meeting or induction is crucial in setting the scene for ongoing working relationships. This is when you start opening up channels of communication with the client, where you make sure that they understand the rules and that they begin to understand the nature of the intervention and your role in it. You are very unlikely to know what the thinking modalities of your client are, therefore you have to try and address all three. In order to do this you need to think carefully about how you are going to work with the client in this session. For instance, showing the client around would tap into kinaesthetic modalities, as would asking them how they feel. Explaining the rules would be auditory and giving a written copy would be visual as long as the client can read (see section on literacy below). A better alternative might be an illustrated set of rules. Showing a short video would be an auditory and visual experience, and if it were of some practical activities, would also tap into the part of the brain that deals with kinaesthetic information.

The language you use will also be important in addressing all three thinking modalities: for instance, if you are trying to get someone's story saying something as simple as 'what did you see, what did you hear, how did you feel?' encompasses all three.

It is worth thinking about all activities to see whether they have an auditory, visual and kinaesthetic component. Group work, for instance, is going to be much more engaging if there is a variety of activities rather than just sitting and talking.

Literacy

It is quite likely that clients will have literacy difficulties. There is evidence that more than one in three offenders has significant literacy and/or numeracy problems and only one in 10 has a reading age of 16 (Davies *et al.* 2004). The term 'literacy' describes the skills of speaking and listening as well as reading and writing. Research has shown that as many as half of all prisoners are dyslexic as opposed to one in 10 of the general population (National Literacy Trust 2004) and the more serious the offence, the more likely the offender is to be dyslexic.

It is important to ensure that information that is written down is made accessible to clients who cannot read. Lewis and Davies (2004) found that the standard rules for Probation Approved Premises (hostels) required a reading age of 16 to fully understand them. Legitimate use of authority is crucial to pro-social modelling and one of the really crucial things for legitimacy is ensuring people know what the rules are. So if the client cannot read the project or institution rules and has no other access to the rules, they cannot reasonably be expected to keep them. If a client cannot read very well they may also need help with things like getting to appointments, following directions, etc.

In spoken communication it is important to pitch your level of communication so that the client can understand. It is easy to slip into jargon, and a client who is well versed in the system may repeat jargon because it is familiar without really understanding it. I recently had a client tell me that he would be an asset in a group because he understood his fellow group members' 'cognitive deficits'. He had attended several Accredited Programmes while in prison and had learned all the jargon; sadly he had little understanding of the meaning of the terms he had learned. Clients may be disempowered by the worker's use of complex language and not feel confident enough to engage in a discussion. A good rule of thumb is to ask yourself whether a word of three syllables or above is understandable.

Some examples of complex and simpler language are shown in Table 8.1 below. These are adapted from the *Literacy and Numeracy Staff Handbook for Use in Approved Premises* (Lewis and Davies 2004).

Many of the guidelines in this section will also help in working with people who do not have a very good grasp of the English language. Pro-social practice with clients with literacy difficulties including dyslexia and

Table 8.1 Examples of specialist and everyday language

Specialist words/phrases	Everyday language
Offence behaviour	The way you do things when you carry out a crime
Pattern of offending	What you have done/your past record behaviour
Different perspectives	Seeing things from other people's point of view
Sequence of events	The order in which things happened or what happened first
Consequences of actions	What happens if you do something
Relapse prevention	Finding ways of avoiding going back to drink/drugs, etc.

limited command of English not only requires the worker to make every effort to ensure that they are communicating clearly, it may also mean helping the client to access resources to improve their literacy.

Summary

Not everyone is like you or me. In order to work pro-socially we need to be aware of this at all times and value everyone's differences and similarities.

When trying to work pro-socially we have to balance the need to encourage people to change themselves and to choose to conform more closely to what is considered to be appropriate (pro-social) behaviour, with taking account of the perspective and the needs of the individual.

We also have to provide a core service of an appropriate standard for everyone, while acknowledging that some people need more or different services and thus avoid a 'one size fits all' approach.

We all see the world through the filter of our preconceptions and stereotypes. We need to become more aware of these, to challenge them and to gain new learning and insights.

We need to reflect on our pro-social practice and ask ourselves whose definition of pro-social we are operating with. Also are we crossing the boundaries of communication that we face due to the differences between our clients and ourselves?

We need to learn to understand and manage the micro-messages about other people that we transmit and also the way in which we interpret micro-messages from others.

If we do not challenge discriminatory behaviour and attitudes we can be seen to be condoning or colluding with it. Challenging is often difficult and uncomfortable but we need to take responsibility ourselves for doing this. Many of the techniques in this book can be helpful, including being assertive, using pro-social feedback and using motivational techniques.

We need to be aware of the different concepts of colour, race, ethnic origin, ethnicity, religion and their importance to individual identity.

In pro-social practice we need to take account of gender, both the client's and ours, because it is such an important part of identity and shapes development so fundamentally.

People have different ways of taking in information. Their predominant way of taking it in may be visual, auditory or kinaesthetic and we need to take account of this.

Many clients may have poor literacy skills. This means that they may find it difficult to understand written materials including instructions, rules, etc. so we have to take account of this in our work with them. It also means that they might not understand complex or jargon words, or complex sentences, and they may not feel confident enough to engage in dialogue with the worker who is using complex language. Therefore we have to use language and concepts that the client can understand so that they can engage fully in the working relationship.

9. Being a pro-social manager: becoming a pro-social organisation

'My manager is really pro-social. She attended the training with us and at every team meeting we discuss a different aspect of our work to see if we can improve it and make it more pro-social. She really practises what she preaches: she is always punctual, if she says she is going to do something she will, if she messes up (which isn't very often) she apologises. She expects a lot of us but she's firm and fair. She bought us all an Easter egg to say "thank you for working so hard", it was a big one too.'

Introduction

The prevailing culture in many organisations means that the manager's attention may be on targets, enforcement and monitoring. However, the effective manager also needs to address the needs of the individuals in the team and equip them to work together (Adair 1987). Just as the client and the worker need to have an empathetic relationship, the staff and the manager also need to have an empathetic relationship within which the manager can help the worker achieve organisational and individual outcomes.

We know from work by McIvor and Barry (2000) and Trotter (1999) that working pro-socially reduces reoffending rates and there is every reason to believe that managing pro-socially will improve the performance of staff. Pro-social modelling is an activity for the whole organisation and the manager plays an absolutely crucial role in introducing, reinforcing and embedding pro-social modelling in the organisation. The pro-social manager not only equips the team members to work pro-socially but also uses the same principles in their own management practice.

This chapter revisits some of the topics already addressed in previous chapters and illustrates how these also apply to the supervision and development of staff and the whole team.

Experience tells me that although pro-social modelling seems like common sense, it is hard to do consistently and 'trickles away' over time if it is not constantly reinforced. In teams where the manager constantly reinforces pro-social practice and is overtly reflective about their own and other people's behaviour, it becomes much more deeply and securely embedded. This chapter provides guidelines for the manager in developing and embedding pro-social modelling in an organisation. It also refers to exercises and instruments to help in this task (Appendices A–E).

The manager as role model

If I had a pound for every time someone said to me on a pro-social modelling course 'I wish my manager would do this course' I would be able to retire. Of course their managers might have already done the training – but if the people on the course have not received the message from their manager that they know what pro-social modelling is and they are committed to it themselves, then the potential to be a positive influence is lost.

Staff in probation hostels (Henry *et al.* 2000) complained that when they were trying to work pro-socially they felt as though they were on view and they had to be on their best behaviour all the time. This is even more the case for managers, who have to demonstrate pro-social behaviour, as far as they can, in their interactions not only with clients but with staff as well. Fortunately they do not have to model perfection all the time because we know that to see someone struggling to do something, and sometimes making mistakes, and then apologising, is less intimidating than seeing someone modelling perfection.

Behaviours and expressions that a manager needs to demonstrate in order to be a positive role model include:

- **Respect for the individual**: 'I am not assuming that everyone is like me. I genuinely want to try and understand other people's view of the world and what is important to them.'

- **Punctuality**: 'I will try to be there on time.'

- **Reliability**: 'If I say I will do something I will, and if I really cannot do it I will say why.'

- **Consistency**: 'I will treat people the same over a period of time as far as I can bearing in mind their individual needs.'

- **Fairness**: 'I will treat everyone according to their needs, but I will try not to ignore, forget or put upon anyone.'

- **Putting things right**: 'If I make a mistake I will say so, put it right and apologise.'

- **Assertiveness**: 'I will aim for a win–win situation, try to be clear about what I am thinking and feeling and what I want to happen, but also try to understand the situation from your point of view.'

The manager as motivator of staff

Like clients, staff also need to be ready, willing and able before they will change or, in a work setting, even engage enthusiastically in everyday practice. The motivational model and techniques described in Chapter 5 apply also to staff. Managers are often unsure how to motivate their staff, and understanding where staff are on the cycle of change can often indicate the best way of moving them forward.

Pre-contemplation: 'I just want a quiet life'
The staff member in pre-contemplation is likely to have been defined as resistant to change. They might say things like 'I just come to work to earn money and I will do what I need to do and no more' or 'what goes around comes around, I've seen it all before' or simply 'I hate this job'. It has to be acknowledged that staff often have more choices than clients; if they really hate the job then they can probably get another one. The manager also has different choices and if there is a significant issue about performance they can institute capability or disciplinary procedures. But often the staff member is not going to leave or be dismissed and as someone said to me on a course recently 'don't write off the dinosaurs yet'.

Managers are often advised to identify performance objectives or set action plans with under-performing members of staff and these can indeed be helpful. However, it is often hard to identify distinct things that need to change; it is more an overall feeling that the staff member could and should be more enthusiastic. If the staff member is not 'ready and willing' to change they probably will not behave differently just because they are given a plan of what they should be doing.

Helping a staff member move from pre-contemplation nearer to action, engaging with the job and developing their practice, requires exactly the same skills and techniques as used with clients. The manager needs to use affirming, listening, open questions, reflection, supporting change talk and supporting self-motivating statements, in order to 'coax, encourage, inform and advise' (DiClemente and Velasquez 2002: 208) staff towards contemplation.

Techniques the manager can use

- **Develop an empathetic relationship** with the staff member, in order to see the world from their point of view. There may be something in the workplace, perceived inequalities in pay, for instance, that is external to the staff member but is affecting their motivation and needs to be addressed or at least acknowledged.

- **Develop discrepancies** to enable the staff member to see the inconsistencies between their long-term goal aspiration and their current behaviour. The staff member who says that they are only two years from retirement and they want a quiet life might also come to see that two years at work is a long time and they could have a more interesting time without being subject to undue pressure.

- **Avoid argument** because argument breeds resistance. It is no good *telling* the member of staff who is near to retirement that you *know* they are capable of more, that they *should* be a role model to younger staff. This is only likely to elicit a response such as 'well, I have done my bit for this organisation and I'm not going to do any more'.

- **Roll with resistance**. By careful empathetic listening, the manager may well be able to engage the staff member in the problem-solving process and move this along by reflecting back to them any self-motivating statements. The demotivated member of staff might say something like 'I really care about the clients but I don't want to stress myself with a lot of new fangled ideas'. This might be an opportunity to reflect the staff member's concern for clients and move them slowly towards thinking about whether some of these 'new fangled' ideas might be in the client's best interests.

- **Develop self-efficacy**. The older and/or more longstanding staff member referred to above probably has a wide repertoire of knowledge and skills and may feel demotivated because their skills are being devalued by changes that are taking place. The role of the manager here might be to help them to value their skills and to see that they have a place in the new world. In some cases new skills may be needed and frequently people are sent on courses as a way of tackling performance and motivation problems. However, unless the manager has done some pre-course preparation with the staff member to enable them to see the point of the training for themselves and to want to do it (i.e. to motivate them) they are likely to be resistant to the training and to learn very little.

(Millner and Rollnick 2002).

The other stages of the cycle of change: 'Well, I suppose while I'm here I might as well make an effort'

Once the staff member has started to think about making a change (contemplation) it is important to support that thinking but not rush them into action. They are much more likely to make real and lasting progress if they are ready for it. As they move around the cycle into decision and action the traditional supervisory and appraisal tools such as performance objectives, action plans, training and coaching are likely to be more effective. However, change and progress may still be fragile and the staff member needs to be affirmed (rewarded) for the efforts that they are making and the difficulties that the changes may present need to be acknowledged.

Ivor had asked to retire at 58, but his application was rejected and he was now facing at least another two years of work and possibly more. At first he was really angry and disappointed and his work and his relationship with colleagues suffered as a result. Ellis, his manager, had a lot of time for him; he was a good solid and reliable worker even if he was not very dynamic. When Ivor first received his knock back Ellis tried to let him know that he was sympathetic. He also tried to tell Ivor that he was pleased to still have him as a member of staff but Ivor just did not want to know. For a couple of weeks Ellis rode out the storm by trying to be kind and sympathetic to Ivor while avoiding getting drawn into Ivor's rants about the unfairness of the system.

At the beginning of the third week Ivor and Ellis had a scheduled supervision meeting. By this time Ivor had calmed down and was just in general state of misery. Ellis started off the meeting by saying to Ivor that he realised that he was deeply disappointed but he still saw Ivor as a valuable member of the team, and now that the first shock had worn off, he would like to talk with him about how he could make the most of the next couple of years.

'I am just so fed up,' said Ivor, 'I was so looking forward to having more time to spend in the garden and with my grandchildren, my wife is retiring and I was looking forward to spending time with her too. I just feel so miserable I can hardly drag myself in in the morning.'

'It's not you lot, or the clients,' he added. 'I have really enjoyed working here and in a way I would have been sorry to leave. But I had got myself all psyched up for a new life.'

'So you are saying you were all ready to move on and now you have been knocked back and you are really disappointed,' said Ellis reflecting both what Ivor had said and what he seemed to be feeling too.

'Yes,' sighed Ivor, 'that is about the sum of it.'

'But sadly we can't do anything about the knock back, so what can we do to make your remaining years here more enjoyable?'

'Dunno,' said Ivor.

'You said a few minutes ago that you really enjoyed working here and in a way you would be sad to leave,' said Ellis.

'Yes, that's true,' said Ivor. 'I really like working with the clients, in fact I was thinking of becoming a volunteer when I retired. Can't do that now.'

Ellis noticed that Ivor brightened up considerably when he talked about the clients although he could see he was slipping into gloom again at the mention of retirement. He interjected quickly before Ivor could get too gloomy: 'So you like the clients so much you though you'd come back and work with them for free then.'

'Well, I suppose every cloud has a silver lining,' said Ivor. 'Now I can work with them and get paid!'

As the meeting continued Ivor regained more of his familiar sense of humour. Ellis acknowledged throughout the meeting that as far as Ivor was concerned whatever they decided would be making the best of a bad job, but he also affirmed the value of Ivor to the team. Ivor responded to Ellis's empathetic style and recognised that there were compensations, particularly continuing to work with the client group that he enjoyed. They went no further than this in the meeting; Ellis didn't discuss targets, action plans or performance at all. He knew Ivor would do at least the minimum required to keep the job ticking over. In fact he felt confident that now Ivor had seen that there were some good things about the job, he would get more of a perspective on the whole situation and there would be time enough to talk about performance then.

The manager as coach: practical steps for helping people to change

Motivational theory tells us that people will not change until they are ready and willing. However, sometimes people may be ready and willing but not able. We saw in Chapter 6 that clients often do not change or develop their behaviour because they do not know how to do this, not because they do not want to, and exactly the same applies to staff.

The suggestions in Chapter 6 for helping clients to change and to learn new skills are equally applicable for helping staff. It is particularly important to remember not to overwhelm staff with too many changes or new things to remember at a time, also to make sure they know what they are aiming for (step 4 of the staged model for helping people to change their behaviour). It is also important to remember to affirm the effort they are making. Coaching staff requires all the empathetic skills that other activities discussed previously.

In square brackets I have identified the stages in the model for helping people to change (Chapter 6).

A few months after Ivor's request for early retirement was knocked back, a temporary specialist secondment was offered to the team. Ivor came to see Ellis. He had settled back down well by now as a member of the team. 'I would really like that job', he said. 'It is right up my street and the timing is right too as the secondment ends at almost the exact time that I am 60.'

Ellis was surprised at his enthusiasm but he could see that the job was indeed very suitable for him. 'The thing that is really concerning me,' said Ivor, 'is that I haven't had an interview for 20 years and I know that even if I am the only applicant, I have to have a meeting with the management committee and that scares me to death. I wondered if you could give me some help?'

'So I am going to lose you after all,' joked Ellis. 'Yes, of course I will try and help you. What is it that worries you?' [1. Identify the specific behaviour that needs to change.]

'I think that I will be very nervous, I will get in a muddle and although I know a lot about this work I will not be able to get it over clearly.'

'So you are saying that you want to manage your nerves so you will be able to think clearly and say what you want to say.' [4. What a competent performance might look like.] Ellis reflected what Ivor had said while also reframing it positively. 'OK. It is quite normal to be nervous you know, I was sick just before my interview for this job, the knack is to manage the nerves and I am sure that you will be able to do that.' [3. Identify the errors in thinking patterns that are leading to inappropriate behaviour.]

'Let's start at the beginning. What do you need to do before you get anywhere near the meeting with the committee?' [2. Break the targeted behaviour down into the smallest possible parts.]

Ivor and Ellis spent about half an hour discussing the interview. With Ellis' help Ivor thought through what he needed to do to prepare for the interview, including anticipating what sort of questions the committee might ask him. Ellis also introduced him to a simple technique for managing his nerves and they talked through those vital few minutes just before and just after he entered the committee room and how he was going to handle them.

As he was leaving Ivor said to Ellis, 'I wish we had done this years ago. I have always hated it when I have to go to management committee meetings to give reports. I don't think I will find it so scary now.' [7. Identify where new skills can be transferred to different situations.]

'Well, interestingly enough you never look scared at the meetings,' said Ellis, 'You always looked really cool and competent, and I am sure you will at this meeting too. [Affirming] Good luck.'

The legitimate use of authority: are we all singing from the same song sheet?

As pro-social practice needs to be undertaken throughout the whole organisation, all staff can be pro-social role models. Therefore it is very important that all the members of the team are delivering a consistent message. This is particularly important when it comes the clarification of roles, legitimate enforcement of rules and the use of rewards. This has been discussed in some length in Chapter 3.

Role boundaries
All staff, including support staff and volunteers need to be clear what role boundaries are. They need to understand that while they can have friendly relationships with clients they are not friends with them; (see Chapter 3). The relationship is not one of equals; workers are trying to steer clients towards a different (pro-social) path. Over-close relationships encourage unrealistic expectations from the client and are likely to give the client the impression that what they are doing or saying is all right. In other words they can be interpreted as collusive. They may also increase the risk of the worker being accused of inappropriate behaviour.

Staff need to keep 'one step removed' from their clients and keep a sense of perspective on what the respective roles are. In some settings this can be very hard for the worker, and the manager can play a very important role in helping them. Ways in which the manager can ensure that staff have a clear sense of role boundaries and what this means in practice include the following.

- **Having a clear sense of their own role boundaries and model this**. In many work settings managers are 'player managers' (Auger and Palmer 2002) – that is, they work with clients alongside the other staff as well as managing the staff. Player managers need to be able to keep the tricky balance between being a friendly colleague and being the manager. One way in which they can do this is to ensure that when they do perform the 'manager' part of their role they do this clearly and competently. Management roles might include setting objectives for the team, ensuring the team members are equipped to carry these objectives out, i.e. they are trained and have the resources they need; and monitoring and evaluating progress. These roles might be carried out through supervision, liaison and negotiation with their own managers (e.g. negotiating with management committees for resources), team meetings or training.

- **Through supervision and at team meetings constantly reiterate with the staff members what the task is**: Staff given the opportunity to discuss their work and their clients can be helped to keep a sense of perspective on the job they are trying to do.

- **Having in place clear guidelines which enable staff to maintain appropriate boundaries and which protect them from risk**: For example, in a hostel setting a guideline which says that staff members should not be alone in a resident's bedroom with the resident.

- **Ensuring that staff have the skills and strategies that they need in order to work pro-socially**. Using strategies such as assertive pro-social feedback allows workers to say important and possibly quite uncomfortable things in a calm and controlled way so that the client can hear. The manager can also use these strategies themselves and encourage staff to use them with one another.

What are the rules: what is negotiable?

Just as the client needs to know what the rules are and what is negotiable, so do the staff. In all but the most disorganised settings, the staff are likely to know what the formal rules are and the expectations on them to enforce these. However, even with formal rules there may be some room for manoeuvre and the task of the manager is to ensure that the 'manoeuvre' is carried out consistently. For instance, in most non-custodial criminal justice settings there are certain behaviours that will lead an offender to be in breach and returned to court. In some cases this decision is unequivocal, for example if an offender repeatedly fails to turn up for a Community Punishment work party he or she will be in breach.

In other cases there is potentially more flexibility. For instance, what do hostel staff do when someone turns up just a few minutes late for curfew with a plausible excuse? One member of staff may overlook it, another may give them a written warning. This would lead to the risk that when the first member of staff is on duty again the resident may think that they can get away with being late back but when the second member of staff is on duty they know they must be back a few minutes early. Also it leads to the risk that another resident, who did receive a written warning for being five minutes late, will think that they are being unfairly treated. In other words the residents are getting an inconsistent message and authority is not being implemented legitimately.

The task of the manager is to ensure that rules are being enforced consistently through monitoring and supervision. If necessary the manager needs to ensure that the staff member understands the reason for the rule being implemented in that way. In the case described above of the late return from curfew, the staff member might think that they are being reasonable in giving the late returner the benefit of the doubt and accepting their excuse. If this was one person and one incident, both in isolation, then this flexibility might be fair and appropriate. However, set in the context of an institution where the rules have to be seen to be applied fairly to everyone, such flexibility is undermining the (pro-social) credibility of the whole team. The staff member can be helped to see that while their desire to be reasonable and compassionate is laudable, in this context it is not appropriate.

The use of rewards

Pro-social modelling is a positive, reward-driven model and staff need to be encouraged to look for every opportunity to reinforce the behaviours that they want to encourage (see Chapter 5 for longer discussion about rewards). Staff need to work together to decide what they want to encourage and how they are going to do this. Developing a common view of what behaviours are to be encouraged (pro-social) is fundamental to working consistently together as a team. Appendix C contains an exercise that can be undertaken at a team meeting. It often helps to tease out the subtleties of different values. Staff may well not entirely agree on what they think is important but they need to be encouraged to try and agree a common approach in order to give a consistent pro-social message.

Managers themselves should also model the use of rewards. Saying thank you and noticing and appreciating good pieces of work is particularly important.

Responsiveness: encouraging staff to treat clients as individuals within a collective system

The manager will need to encourage staff to think about how they will use their learning in interactions with clients and make sure that they are responsive to individual clients' differences and similarities (see Chapter 8).

For instance, the manager needs to encourage staff to do the following:

- **Treat clients as individuals.** Are they genuinely doing this and taking care to try and see the world from their client's point of view?

- **Take account of different cultural values.** This is a difficult one because the underpinning values of pro-social modelling are generated within a predominantly white euro-centric society. However, even if the ultimate message is 'it is not acceptable to do that here', this message needs to also carry acknowledgment of and respect for other cultures.

- **Avoid stereotypes about what is 'normal'** (for example, what 'normal family life' is).

- **Take account of the different experiences of males and females.** In criminal justice and other fields, most of the research which informs work with clients has been undertaken on groups of men and the findings often do not translate to women. In some fields such as education there is an increasing understanding of the different needs of girls and boys; however, it is important to check the basis of evidence for different ways of working.

- **Take account of people's different learning styles.**

- **Use language and concepts that take account of the client's thinking and listening abilities and/or their grasp of the English language** (i.e. are there simpler ways of conveying concepts such as 'offending behaviour' or 'relapse prevention').

Responsiveness: treating staff as individuals within a collective system

Just as staff need to be responsive to the individual similarities and differences of clients, managers must take account of the similarities and differences of staff members. Things to take account of might include:

- **Key information for all staff** (usually given at induction). The organisation's underlying values, how these are formalised in equality policies. Expectations of behaviour. What to do if confronted by racist, sexist or other discriminatory behaviour. How they can report any incidents, what support they can expect, where you as manager stand on this.

- **Isolation and support of staff.** Staff who are in a minority in an organisation can feel isolated. The manager must take account of this and ensure that they are aware of the support available for them.

- **Equality of opportunity to benefit from supervision, appraisal and development which focuses on work-based issues and uses evidence to justify conclusions.** Her Majesty's Inspector of Probation Thematic Inspection *Report Towards Racial Equality* (Calderbank and Flaxington 2000) followed other research in finding that black probation staff had often not been supervised as well or as frequently as white staff. In particular there was evidence that white managers lacked the confidence to tackle anti-discriminatory practice and the promotion of equal opportunities constructively. Also managers could be experienced but unaware or insensitive on issues of cultural differences and race. More recently the Morris Report (2004), examining the Metropolitan Police Service, found significant weaknesses in the way that staff who are 'different' are managed. Morris said: (2004: 11) 'we are concerned that some managers lack the confidence to manage black and minority ethnic officers without being affected by their race'. Also 'we have received information that managers lack confidence in managing other issues of difference whether gender, disability, sexual orientation or faith'.

  There is no reason to think that the Probation Service or the Metropolitan Police Service are any different from other organisations in this respect. All managers need to develop the skills, knowledge and confidence to manage staff of a different race and/or culture to their own, or different in other ways such as sexuality or gender. Training and development on managing diversity needs to be provided at an organisational level but it is also incumbent upon individuals to take responsibility for their own development through (for example) enquiry, reading and the supervisory process.

Developing and embedding pro-social practice

Pro-social modelling is an all day and every day activity, which is reinforced overtly and covertly by every bit of practice. There are, however, skills, techniques and strategies that staff should be familiar with which will help them to work pro-socially:

- Using interpersonal skills to develop empathy (Chapter 2).
- Being positive and solution-focused (Chapter 2).
- Being clear about roles (Chapter 3).
- Being clear about rules (Chapter 3).
- Appropriate (legitimate) use of rewards and sanctions (Chapter 3).
- Interacting assertively (Chapter 4).
- Pro-social feedback (Chapter 4).
- Using motivational techniques (Chapter 5).
- Helping people to change by coaching and modelling (Chapter 6).
- Taking a systematic approach to problem-solving (Chapter 7).
- Being responsive to the needs of the individual (Chapter 8).

There is no substitute for a good training course to introduce a team or individuals to pro-social practice (see details of pro-social modelling training at the end of the book). The impact will be most powerful when it is delivered to the whole team if possible, including the manager. This allows the team to examine their values and their practice as part of the training.

Undertaking an audit of the whole team

Appendix A is a pro-social audit. This is a **whole team** activity that involves the team in identifying what they mean by pro-social behaviour and then auditing the work place according to how well those behaviours are taking place. It is a fairly lengthy exercise and would be suitable for part of an away day (although guidelines are given for managing the time). I have used it extensively with teams who have always found the discussion of what they mean by pro-social behaviour extremely useful, and the audit gives them a base line against which to chart their progress. This is followed by an Action Planning exercise based on the audit (Appendix B).

Assessment and development of individual practice

Appendix D can be used as a model to develop a checklist of your own to use in a variety of ways: This checklist is based on those developed for quality assurance (QA) for the Enhanced Community Punishment and Approved Premises Pathfinders (pilot). My experience with the QA forms developed for the pathfinder was that if they became longer than about one page no one could keep track of what they are trying to observe so

I have made this model form very short. However, in doing this some of the fine detail is lost and you (the manager) might want to expand some sections of it: if you were concentrating on a particular aspect of pro-social practice (motivating the client) for example. Expanding a section with the whole team or one person could become a development exercise in its own right.

Uses for the assessment form include:

- **Self-assessment/development** The checklist can be used by individuals to reflect on their own pro-social practice.

- **Peer assessment/development** The checklist can be used to observe another's practice in order to identify what they are doing well and what they need to work towards changing.

- **Supervision** The checklist can be used as the basis of supervision. It can be completed using observation by the manager, by the supervisee, by peers or a combination of these. It can also be completed by observation of video taped practice if this is available.

- **To develop a benchmark** The checklist can be used to establish a benchmark against which the development of practice can be measured. For instance, before a team undertook pro-social modelling training they could assess themselves against the checklist and then collate the results. Then after training they could assess themselves to see if they had made progress. (This is a rather crude process as it is conceivable that as the team gains understanding of what pro-social practice is they assess themselves as doing less well rather than better.)

  An alternative might be to get an outside observer with a high level of understanding of pro-social practice to assess the group. In this case rather than using the 1–5 scale the observer could just count every time they see the pro-social behaviour described: for instance, every time they see the staff member(s) use positive and solution-focused language. The observer could then repeat the counting after training and assess whether the number of pro-social interactions had increased.

Reinforcing pro-social organisational modelling

The importance of pro-social organisational modelling has already been referred to in Chapter 1. At a senior level managers can play a significant role in developing and enforcing pro-social modelling by demonstrating wholehearted support, taking an interest in and attending training, modelling the behaviours they are encouraging, e.g. punctuality, reliability, honesty and respect for colleagues. Senior managers and their actions are very visible and therefore are role models. Pro-social practice can be demonstrated both face-to-face and in other ways such as written communications. Newsletters can demonstrate inclusivity and diversity by a careful choice of topics, contributors and pictures.

Policies and procedures also demonstrate a pro-social organisation. The fairness and transparency of discipline and grievance, diversity and harassment and bullying policies and whether they are implemented consistently and fairly are key indicators of pro-social practice. Front line managers need to make sure that not only their face-to-face behaviour reinforces it, but also letters to clients, posters on the wall, the way clients are treated in the waiting room, the way the phone is answered, etc.

Developing a pro-social physical environment

The physical environment can give some powerful messages about the way in which the organisation regards its clients. Birmingham Prison is a forbidding Victorian building surrounded by high walls. Despite a great deal of new building, the overall impression is very scary. Induction to a prison must be one of the most frightening and bewildering experiences that most of us can imagine. The prison has undergone a massive culture change in the last four years under the leadership of the Governor Mike Shann. One of the places where this is evident is in the induction centre and the first night wing, which is where prisoners stay while they are risk assessed. Both of these are still unmistakably part of a prison, but the use of bright non-institutional colours, decent chairs in waiting rooms, and dozens of notices on the walls with useful information convey a message that the incoming prisoner is not going to be treated as a number. These are in addition to the notices that are in all prisons nowadays stating the intention to treat people with decency and to oppose racial and other abuse.

Next time you walk into your office or other work place try to put yourself in the shoes of a client:

- How might they be feeling? Nervous, frightened, angry, miserable?
- Can they find the place and work out easily how to get in?
- What does your reception say to them, what are the messages on the wall?
- Do you have tidy, up to date and colourful notices that take account of the fact that not everyone can read?

- Is the reception area fairly tidy, is there something for them to do while they wait?

- Do they have access to a drink of water and a toilet?

- Do you tell them how long they are going to have to wait?

- Do you have more notices saying what people can do than ones that say 'Clients should not ...', 'Clients are forbidden to ...', etc?

All these things give a powerful message about your organisation and the way you regard your clients. Does the environment convey the messages you want it to convey? For instance, you are safe here, we can help you, we care about you and the other clients, everyone is welcome, etc.

The client who feels respected and decently treated is much more likely to come to you in a receptive frame of mind. Conversely the client who feels alienated and mistreated is much less likely to work with you and more likely to be hostile and aggressive.

Constructive conflict management within the team

Agree and use ground rules before conflict erupts

Use a team meeting to devise a set of team ground rules; you could start with any ground rules used in the work place (e.g. in group work, programmes, hostels, etc.) and see whether they apply to you as a team. Encourage the team to think of situations where they have been unhappy or concerned and to identify a ground rule that might have helped.

When you have agreed a set of ground rules post them around the office where they are visible. Encourage team members to refer to these (pro-socially) when something is concerning them (and model this yourself). For example:

I am concerned that we are not singing from the same song sheet in our work together. When we work together running the group you often chip in when I am trying to develop a discussion, but I feel that what you say cuts short the discussion and leaves me floundering. We have a ground rule about trying to be open about things that are concerning us and not letting things fester so I have plucked up the courage to say this to you and I would really like us to discuss this and try and sort it out. (Team member)

Or

I am concerned that although we all agreed to come to this meeting today having prepared a case to discuss, only three of us have done this. Last week we talked about how we could improve our practice and we agreed a set of ground rules to help us to feel safe doing this; this included trying to be open and honest and also creating a non-blaming atmosphere. I am concerned that we don't seem to have got off to a very good start. Is there a problem here? (Manager)

This kind of approach is more assertive, less accusatory and more likely to lead to an open discussion.

Encourage and model pro-social feedback

Using the principles of pro-social feedback equips you and the team to address potentially difficult issues in a way that is as constructive as possible:

1 Make sure you both know what you are talking about.
2 Make sure you are describing the behaviour, not the personality.
3 Say what you liked/did not like (use 'I' statements) and explain why you liked/did not like the behaviour (its impact on you/others).
4 Talk about what might be different.
5 Do not overdo it.

If conflict flares

The above principles still apply, i.e. use ground rules and pro-social feedback.

Helping people to work together: critical incident analysis

Critical incident analysis (Appendix E) outlines a method of unpicking an incident in such a way that the quest is for lessons to be learned and not to apportion blame. This can be used with staff to unpick an incident with a client or within the staff group.

Summary

Managers are a very important force for modelling, developing and embedding pro-social practice.

The manager should pay attention to:

* Modelling as a role model and as a coach.
* Legitimacy.
* Responsiveness.
* Pro-social practice.
* Pro-socially managing conflict.
* Developing a pro-social environment.

Most of the models suggested for being a pro-social manager are the same as the models for developing pro-social practice in the rest of this book.

When motivating staff members the manager needs to understand where the staff member is on the cycle of change and choose appropriate strategies for that stage.

Managers must help team members to develop their skills.

Team members need to be 'singing from the same song sheet'. This means they should be aware of role boundaries, what the rules are and what is negotiable and how to use rewards to encourage positive behaviour change.

Managers need to ensure that team members are responsive to the individuality of their clients. Managers must also be responsive to the individual needs of their team members. They need to make sure they have the skills and confidence to manage, support and develop a diverse staff group equitably.

Managers need to be constantly developing and reinforcing pro-social practice otherwise it becomes eroded.

Managers play a crucial role in ensuring that the whole organisation models pro-social practice.

The physical environment gives important messages to clients about the way the organisation regards them, which can have a big impact on their willingness to engage with the worker.

Mangers need to manage conflict within the team and also to help and support team members who have experienced conflict to debrief and learn from the experience in a 'no blame' environment.

Appendices: Exercises to develop and embed pro-social modelling in teams

The exercises in appendices A, B, C and E are all adapted from *Pro-social Modelling: Reinforcement Strategies for Managers* (Cherry 2004b). Available from MPTC. e-mail: info@mptc.org.uk

Permission is granted to photocopy without change Appendices A to E, pages 158–177, for private use only.

Appendix A
Pro-social audit of the workplace

Introduction

The point of this exercise is to undertake a pro-social audit, and to encourage staff to think about what pro-social modelling looks like in practice. This exercise should take two hours but can take a very long time if you go into too much detail, so you may have to prioritise the activities you choose to audit. In this case choose those that are most symbolic of a pro-social environment, for instance in almost every setting the first contact, reception and/or induction is very important.

Auditing 'manager to staff' interactions is very important but can feel very risky so if relations between yourself and the staff are difficult this may not be the right way to tackle it.

The instructions provided on the next pages can be photocopied and given to everyone. I have provided an example of one page filled in. This is meant as an illustration of the level of detail required, not as definitive answers.

This audit gives an overall picture of the functioning of the team and the project. Some of the behaviours described will inevitably be individual ones and you can only get an impression of whether they are taking place during this audit, but you could follow up some of the more individual points by using the quality assurance instrument provided in Appendix D.

Resources needed

- Photocopies of the instructions given below for the pro-social audit, one for each team member.
- Photocopies of the blank pro-social audit sheet. Each sheet should have one of the following headings:

- Staff to clients
- Staff to staff
- Managers to staff
- Clients to clients
- Other
- Environment.

You will need two or three sheets for each category.

Employment, training and education example

Activities that take place	Pro-social behaviours (and conditions) related to these activities	1	2	3	4	5
Staff to clients						
Visit to office	Friendly greeting as soon as they enter office Explanation from receptionist of any delays, whether interviewer knows they are there, etc.					
Initial meeting	Clear explanation of the process Meeting held in a setting with no interruptions Careful listening Clear explanation of key information Provision of information in an accessible form (not just written) Checking of understanding Prioritising of information given (to avoid overload at this stage)					
Referral and visit to partner agency (e.g. Apex)	Clear explanation of where to go and how to get there Employment adviser knows s/he is coming and is ready to meet them Clear explanation of task and process for the meeting Checking understanding Information sharing between agencies made transparent Expectations, rules, etc. made transparent Client given a chance to ask questions Consistent reinforcement of pro-social attitudes and behaviour					

Pro-social Audit: Instructions

Please read the instructions carefully and ensure that you work through them systematically; do not move on to the next stage until you are absolutely sure that you have completed the previous stage.

A: (in small groups)
Identify as many activities as possible that involve interactions between people, under the following headings. Include both formal and informal activities.

Staff to clients:
e.g. Reception:
Taking part in group work including accredited programmes
Basic skills tutoring
One-to-one sessions (key work/case management/PSR writing)
Everyday contacts on the wing (prisons)

Staff to staff:
e.g. Handover
Referral of a case
Co-working

Managers to staff:
e.g. Chairing a meeting
Supervision
Appraisal interview
Allocating work

Clients to clients:
e.g. Eating together (hostels)
Working together (e.g. ECP)
Group work

As a whole staff group formulate a common list; enter these onto the first column of the pro-social modelling pro-forma (it is usually only practical to work with three or four things under each heading so decide which is the most important – for instance, initial contacts are always important in setting a pro-social climate).

B: (in different small groups)
Imagine the perfect pro-social setting, and identify the pro-social behaviours that you would expect to see under each sub-heading. Fill these in on the pro-forma provided.

Also imagine the perfect 'physical environment' (see section on pro-social environment in Chapter 9 for guidance).

C: Before you move on to the next stage go back and check that:

1 You have described **behaviours that are identifiable** (with the exception of the physical environment).
2 Looking at the section on physical environment are there any examples that would lead to the physical environment that you describe? (For instance, if you have said in a hostel that there should be evidence on the walls of resident activities, you could put a behaviour in the 'staff to resident' category about encouraging residents to produce visual material and making it possible for them to put it on the walls.)

You are aiming to have a detailed list of desirable pro-social behaviours that you can all understand and recognise, and therefore work towards. Do not worry if the list is repetitious.

As a whole group agree what to put on the final copy of the pro-social audit.

D: After discussion as a group, audit your workplace/team using the criteria that you have devised together.

The levels are:
1 *Poor*: very little or no evidence that pro-social behaviour is taking place.
2 *Need for improvement*: some pro-social behaviour is taking place but inconsistently and/or not frequently enough.
3 *Adequate*: there is a reasonable amount of pro-social behaviour taking place but it is still not very consistent across the staff group and across all situations.
4 *Good*: The staff group are using pro-social behaviours most of the time and are becoming self-policing, i.e they recognise when they have not

been pro-social and publicly correct themselves. Staff are giving one another pro-social feedback.

5 *Excellent*: The staff group are consistently using pro-social behaviour and are supporting one another pro-socially. It is clear that the pro-social behaviour is having a positive impact on the staff, residents and hostel life.

E: Use the audit to form an action plan (Appendix B) for the areas that you need to work on as individuals and as a staff group.

Note: You could also audit interactions outside your immediate workplace/ team, e.g. with case managers, partners, etc. The design of the audit only allows you to audit communications from your team outwards, not vice versa.

Pro-social Audit

Date of initial audit....................................

Activities that take place in the workplace/team	Pro-social behaviours (or conditions) related to these activities	1	2	3	4	5

Appendix B:
Action planning using the pro-social audit

Introduction

This exercise follows on from the pro-social audit. Both audit and action plan can then be reviewed at a later date.

Resources needed
Photocopies of pro-social action plan that follows.

Stage 1: (all together, use a flip chart) Start by listing all the things that scored 1, 2 or 3; list both the key activity (e.g. handover) and the behaviours within that activity.

Stage 2: Decide on the order of importance of your list. The priorities will be:

(a)   The activities that are most likely to be an opportunity to influence clients (or colleagues) positively to behave more pro-socially. For instance (using the example in the introduction to Appendix A) in the 'staff to clients' category you might have several low scores on behaviours (or conditions) under 'initial meeting' and also under 'referral to other agencies'. You might decide that as an 'initial meeting' sets the tone for the client's whole contact with the organisation and a limited number of people will attend life skills sessions, your priority is to work on initial meeting.

(b)   Behaviours (or conditions) that consistently score low. For instance you might find that often you have scored 'clear explanations of task and process of meetings' quite low. This might indicate that you need to do some work on introductions to meetings and interviews.

(c)   Anything else you think is important.

Stage 3: Use the information above to write your action plan. There is no point in doing this exercise unless you are going to use the plan so make sure that it is SMART:

Specific: Be clear what it is that you are planning to do e.g. not just 'work on introductions to meetings and interviews' but 'work on introductions to meetings in order to devise a way of ensuring that we do not forget to tell the client what we are going to do and why and check that they have understood'.

Measurable: Ensure that when you have completed your action point you will be able to tell that you have done it. In the example above you might end up with an interview checklist. You could also revisit the audit.

Achievable: You are busy people with limited time and resources so be realistic about what you can work on; some things might have to be parked for a future date. Break big areas into a series of small steps.

Relevant/realistic: See above, make sure you prioritise.

Timed: Write in review times.

Note: make sure you know who is going to lead on each area.

Pro-social Action Plan

Date:

SMAR(T) Action:	Person who is going to make sure it happens	Review date

Appendix C
Rewards, sanctions and values

Introduction

This exercise provides an opportunity for the whole team to check they are 'singing from the same song sheet'. It will take approximately 90 minutes; however, you could ask people to fill in stage 2 in their own time, in which case it will take approximately 45 minutes.

Resources needed
Photocopies of summary that follows.

Stage 1: What do we want to reward and how are we going to do it?

(In pairs/threes)

A. List behaviour that you want to encourage. Think of small examples of behaviour. Remember that clients often need encouraging and rewarding for doing things that you might think they should be doing anyway. Write your list on the left hand side of a piece of flip chart paper (landscape).

B. Swap your list with another pair/trio and on the right hand side of the sheet of paper that you now have, list all the rewards you can think of, linking them to the behaviours on the left wherever possible. Remember: think small, 'please' and 'thank you' is a reward and research in South Yorkshire Hostels (Henry *et al.* 2000) showed that it was the little things like these that the residents really valued.

Obviously rewards have to fit into the constraints of project rules, organisation rules, National Standards etc.

You may not all feel comfortable with some of the suggestions that come up and we are going to return to them after the next exercise.

Stage 2: Thinking about our own values and the values of the work we are doing

On your own, answer the following questions (you are going to discuss them as a group).

1 What is my role? Describe in a few words not your job title but what you really think you do. Chris Trotter (1999) when talking about work with the involuntary client says that is very important to be clear and open with clients about what your role is in order to have an honest and empathetic relationship with them.

2 What is my best hope for the work we do here?

3 What is a reasonable expectation?

4 What behaviour or attitudes are non-negotiable?

5 What is negotiable?

6 What do I find tricky? What do we have to do/reinforce here that does not sit very comfortably with my own beliefs/values?

7 What do we find tricky? What do we find difficult to do consistently here?

8 Who are our stakeholders? Who do we have to keep happy in order to stay in business?

Stage 3:

Taking each heading at a time, discuss as a group your answers to the questions. It is not always easy or comfortable discussing values and you may have to agree to disagree. However, the discussion should help you to relate your values to the work that you are doing.

Stage 4:

A: Return to the previous exercise on what you want to reward and how. Hopefully by now you will all be able to subscribe to a common set of behaviours to reward and rewards. Even if you are not 100 per cent convinced of the merits of everything agreed the discussion should help you to understand why you as a group have arrived at the list and allow you to go along with it at least until it gets reviewed.

B: Discuss how you are going to ensure consistency.

Summary

Behaviours/attitudes that we want to encourage	Rewards that we are going to use

Appendix D
Pro-social modelling:
assessment of individual practice

Introduction

On the following page is a short checklist which can be used as a model to develop one of your own to use in a variety of ways. This checklist is based on those developed for quality assurance (QA) for the Enhanced Community Punishment and Approved Premises Pathfinders (various authors 2003/4 unpublished).

My experience with the QA forms developed for the pathfinder (Cherry 2004 unpublished) was that if they exceeded about one page no one could keep track of what they are trying to observe so I have made this model form very short. However, in doing this some of the fine detail is lost and you (the manager) might want to expand some sections of it if you are concentrating on a particular aspect of pro-social practice (motivating the client, for instance) Expanding a section with the whole team or one person could become a development exercise in its own right.

Uses for the assessment form

- **Self-assessment/development:** The checklist can be used by an individual to reflect on their own pro-social practice.
- **Peer assessment/development:** The checklist can be used to observe another's practice in order to identify what they are doing well and what they need work towards changing.
- **Supervision:** The checklist can be used as the basis of supervision. It can be used by the manager, by the supervisee or by peers or a combination of these. It can also be completed by observation of video taped practice if this is available.
- **To develop a benchmark:** The checklist can be used to develop a benchmark against which the development of practice can be measured. For instance, before a team undertakes pro-social modelling training each individual could assess themselves against the checklist and then collate the results. Then after training they could assess themselves to see if they had made progress. (This is a rather crude process as it is conceivable that as the team gain understanding of what pro-

social practice is they assess themselves as doing less well rather than better.)

An alternative might be to get an outside observer with a high level of understanding of pro-social practice to assess the group. In this case rather than using the 1–5 scale I would suggest that the observer could just count every time they see the pro-social behaviour described: for instance, every time they see the staff member(s) use positive and solution-focused language. The observer could then repeat the counting after training and assess whether the number of pro-social interactions had increased.

Resources needed
Photocopies of following pro-social modelling assessment.

Pro-social modelling: assessment of practice

The worker is scored for the extent to which they are achieving the statement on a scale of 1–5. There is also a 'not applicable' category.

N/A	1	2	3	4	5
Not Applicable	Poor	Need for improvement	Adequate	Good	Excellent

a	Addressing the client by their correct name	N/A	1	2	3	4	5
b	Being on time	N/A	1	2	3	4	5
c	Using appropriate interpersonal skills to develop empathy with the client (this includes trying to respond appropriately to any problems engaging the client such as being reluctant to talk)	N/A	1	2	3	4	5
d	Demonstrating optimism that the client can learn and change	N/A	1	2	3	4	5
e	Using positive and solution-focused language	N/A	1	2	3	4	5
f	Being clear with the client about the role of the worker	N/A	1	2	3	4	5
g	Being clear about the rules and the consequences of breaking the rules	N/A	1	2	3	4	5
h	Being open and consistent in the way they treat clients and apply the rules	N/A	1	2	3	4	5
i	Using constructive feedback to challenging anti-social/pro-criminal behaviour and attitudes	N/A	1	2	3	4	5
j	Seeking out and use opportunities to praise or affirm positive behaviour (however small scale)	N/A	1	2	3	4	5
k	Seeking out and use opportunities to praise or affirm efforts to engage with change even if the actual achievement is small	N/A	1	2	3	4	5

l	Using constructive feedback to praise and reinforce desirable (pro-social) behaviours and attitudes	N/A	1	2	3	4	5
m	Being overtly reflective on own behaviour (including behaviour which is not as pro-social as it should be)	N/A	1	2	3	4	5
n	Using motivational techniques	N/A	1	2	3	4	5
o	Taking a systematic approach to problem solving	N/A	1	2	3	4	5
p	Actively helping people to learn new skills by modelling and coaching	N/A	1	2	3	4	5
q	Using language and concepts that the client can understand	N/A	1	2	3	4	5
r	Challenging discriminatory attitudes and behaviour	N/A	1	2	3	4	5

Appendix E
Working pro-socially
together: critical incident analysis

Introduction

This format can be used for debriefing after an incident or for practice development (in other words the incident does not have to be truly critical but may be one which was tricky or just interesting). It can be used to unpick incidents that have gone well or not so well.

This format is not designed to be used as part of a disciplinary process and the emphasis is strongly on **not** apportioning blame.

It is helpful to agree ground rules before starting this exercise. Please remember to give one another pro-social feedback. The exercise will take 30–45 mins.

Step 1: Key players in the incident describe their perception of what took place, concentrating at this stage on **facts not interpretations** as much as possible. Start with the people most closely involved. Make sure everyone has a clear picture of what happened but do not go into more detail than necessary at this stage.

Step 2: Looking back at the incident try to complete an iceberg diagram for everyone involved: in other words what were the parties thinking and feeling and how did this relate to their behaviour (if it is helpful, draw a series of triangles, one for each party, on a flip chart, and fill in the three points for each person). Do not spend too long on this, just enough to try and see some of the underlying reasons for the behaviour.

Step 3: Ask the key player(s) to imagine that they could wind the clock back and with hindsight replay the incident. What would they do the same and what would they do differently?

Do not allow them to be unduly critical of themselves. It is much easier to be wise after the event than in the middle of it. Remind them this is not about attributing blame but about learning and applying the learning next time.

Step 4: When the key player(s) have had their say, ask the rest of the group for their comments. Again, do not allow them to be unduly critical but encourage them to come up with positive and specific suggestions for what might have been done differently (or what should be done the same).

Step 5: As a group list the learning points resulting from this exercise. Remember that there will be procedural, organisational learning points as well as personal ones.

Training and consultancy in pro-social practice

Training and consultancy for practitioners and managers in pro-social modelling and many other topics is available from:

MPTC
5th Floor King Edward House
135 New Street
Birmingham B2 4QJ
0121 248 6325
website: www.mptc.org.uk

MPTC also publishes various manuals and booklets such as:

- *Pro-social Modelling: Reinforcement Strategies for Managers*
- *Introducing Pro-social Modelling: A Handbook for Hostel Staff*
- *Introducing Pro-social Modelling: A Handbook for Prison Staff*
- *LiHMO: Living Here, Moving On. A Group Work Programme for Hostel Residents*
- *From Murmur to Murder: Working with Racially Motivated Offenders*

This book is very much a work in progress and the author welcomes comments to:

sally@mptc.org.uk
sally.cherry@btinternet.com

Recommended reading

While developing my thinking about pro-social practice there were some books that I found particularly helpful. These are all, to an extent, 'how to books': they are all practical and readable and I consider them to be an essential part of the reflective pro-social practitioner's bookshelf.

First and foremost is Chris Trotter's *Working with Involuntary Clients* (1999). Chris Trotter has been in the forefront of developing research and practice with this client group. In his book he draws on examples from probation and from child protection, but he points out that the principles are relevant to a range of different workers and clients. His book takes a different angle from my book and he describes an integrated approach that contains:

- Role clarification
- Pro-social modelling and enforcements
- Problem solving
- Relationships

The principles are much the same as what I have called pro-social practice. Trotter is an academic and there is a good deal of reference to research to back up what he says. Trotter has also published a more recent book, *Helping Abused Children and their Families* (2004). Equally readable, it is based on a research study with this group and develops his effective practice model further. It is worth reading even if you are not working with abused children as it has wide general applications.

Another readable and useful book is Miller and Rollnick's *Motivational Interviewing* (2002). The first part of the book is about the theory and practice of motivational interviewing. It includes a section on learning motivational interviewing. The second part is written by a variety of authors and looks at applications of motivational interviewing in a range of settings. Wherever you work you are likely to find something relevant to your setting here.

I find Solution-Focused Therapy extremely appealing because it is client centred and ethical, it is positive and forward looking, it tends to yield results quickly and it is easy to apply to everyday practice. Bill O'Connell's book of the same name (1998) is an easy read and explains this way of working really well. I have recommended this book to many colleagues and they have all found something useful in it.

References

Ameli, S.R., Elahi, M. and Merali, A. (2004) *Across the Muslim Divide*. London: Islamic Human Rights Commission.

Adair, J. (1987) *Effective Team Building*. London: Pan.

Augar, P. and Palmer, J. (2002) *The Rise of the Player Manager: How Professionals Manage While They Work*. London: Penguin.

Back, K. and Back, K. (1991) *Assertiveness at Work*. London: McGraw Hill.

Bandler, R. and Grinder, (1975) *The Structure of Magic 2*. London: Science and Behaviour Books.

Bandura, A. (1977) *Social Learning Theory*. New York: Prentice-Hall.

Berne, E. (1964) *Games People Play*. London: Penguin.

Bottoms, A. and Rex, S. (1998) Pro-social modelling and legitimacy: their potential contribution to effective practice, in Rex, S. and Maltravers, A. *op. cit.*

Bottoms, A., Gelsthorpe, L. and Rex, S. (eds.) (2001) *Community Penalties: Change and Challenges*. Devon: Willan.

Bottoms, A. (2004) *Compliance and Community Penalties*, in Bottoms, Gelsthorpe and Rex *op cit*.

Bonta, J. (2002) Paper for the Probation Interventions Conference (unpublished).

Bonta, J. and Rugge, T. (2004) *Case Management in Manitoba Probation*. Manitoba: Department of Justice and Corrections.

Bridges, A. (2005) *I am Not a Racist But ... An Inspection of National Probation Service Work with Racially Motivated Offenders*. London: Her Majesty's Inspector of Probation.

Calderbank, L. and Flaxington, F. (2000) *Thematic Inspection Report Towards Race Equality*. London: Her Majesty's Inspector of Probation.

Chapman, T. and Hough, M. (1998) *Evidence Based Practice: A Guide to Effective Practice*. London: Home Office.

Cherry, S. (2004a) *Living Here Moving On (LiHMO) A group work programme for offenders in hostels*. Birmingham: MPTC.

Cherry, S. (2004b) *Pro-social Modelling: Reinforcement Strategies for Managers*. Birmingham: NPD/MPTC.

Chigwada-Bailey (2003) *Black Women's Experience of Criminal Justice*. Winchester: Waterside Press.

Chui, W.H. and Nellis, M. (eds) (2003) *Moving Probation Forward*. Harlow: Pearson.

Collett, P. (2004) *The Book of Tells*. London: Bantam Books.

CRE (2004) *Categories for Ethnic Monitoring*. London: Commission for Racial Equality.

Covey, S. (1999) *Seven Habits of Highly Effective People*. London: Simon and Schuster.

Davies, K., Lewis, J., Byatt, J., Purvis, E., and Cole, B. (2004) *An Evaluation of the Literacy Demands of General Offending Behaviour Programmes HO Research Findings 233*. London: Home Office.

Di Clemente and Velasquez (2002) in Miller, W. and Rollnick, S. (2002) *Motivational Interviewing*. New York: Guildford.

Dowden, C. and Andrews, D.A. (2004) The importance of staff practice in delivering effective correctional treatment: A meta-analytic review of correctional practice. *International Journal of Offender Therapy and Comparative Criminology*, 48, 203–214.

Farrall, S. (2004) *Rethinking What Works With Offenders*. Devon: Willan.

Fenwick, S. (2005) Achieving change in Whitemoor Segregation Unit. *Prison Service Journal* 158 March 2005 9–11.

Fleet, F. and Annison, J. (2003) *In Support of Effectivess: Facilitating Participation and Sustaining Change.*

Fuller, C. and Taylor, P. (2003) *Toolkit of Motivational Skills*. London: National Probation Directorate.

Fuller, C. (2004) *Systematic Motivational Work in Approved Premises*. London: National Probation Directorate.

Foster, S. (2003) *Approved Premises: Results of a Snapshot Survey 2003. Home Office RDS Findings 230* London: Home Office.

Gast, L. and Taylor, P. (1998) *Influence and Integrity*. Birmingham: MPTC.

Gast, L. et. al. *From Murmur to Murder*. Birmingham: MPTC.

Gelsthorpe, L. (1998) Reflections on a workshop: accommodating social difference: pro-social modelling and legitimacy in probation practice, in Rex and Maltravers (1998) *op. cit.*

Gelsthorpe, L. (2001) Accountability: differences and diversity in the delivery of community programmes, in Bottoms, Gelsthorpe and Rex *op. cit.*

Ginsberg J., Mann, R., Rotgers, F. and Week, J. (2002) Motivational interviewing in criminal justice populations, in Miller and Rollnick *op. cit.*

Harper, R. and Handy, S. (2002) An evaluation of motivational interviewing as a method of intervention with clients in a probation setting. *British Journal of Social Work* 30: 393–400.

Harris, T. (1970) *I'm OK, You're OK*. London: Pan.

Hearnden, I. and Hough, M. (2004) *Race and the Criminal Justice System*. London: The Institute for Criminal Policy Research School of Law, King's College.

Henry, C., Holdsworth, A., Harrison, A. (2000) *Evaluating the Implementation of Pro-social Modelling in South Yorkshire Hostels (Approved Premises)* London: National Probation Service for England and Wales.

Hollis, V., Goodman, M. and Cross, I. (2003) *Prison Population Brief 2003. Home Office Research Findings*. London: Home Office.

Hough, M., Clancy, A., McSweeny, T. and Turnbull, P. (2003) *The Impact of Drug Treatment and Testing Orders: two year reconviction rates. Home Office Research Findings 184*. London: Home Office.

Huesmann, L.R. and Podolski, C.L. (2003) Punishment: a psychological perspective, in McConville, S. *op. cit.*

Jefferson, T. (1997) Masculinities and crime, in *The Oxford Handbook of Criminology 2nd Edition*. Oxford: Clarendon Press.

Kay, J. and Gast, L. (1998) *Murder to Murder: Working with Racially Motivated and Racist Offenders*. Birmingham: MPTC.

Kemshall, H. and Canton, R. (2003) *The Effective Management of Programme Attrition: A report for the NPS (Welsh Region)* Leicester: DeMontford University.

Kemshall, H. *et. al.* (2004a) *Dimensions of Difference in Alternatives to Prison*. Devon: Willan.

Kemshall, H. *et. al.* (2004b) Beyond programmes: organizational and cultural issues in the implementation of What Works, in Mair, G. *op. cit.*

Kendall, K. (2004) Dangerous thinking: a critical history of correctional cognitive behaviouralism, in Mair, G. *op. cit.*

Laurance, J. (2003) *Pure Madness: How Fear Drives the Mental Health System*. Oxford: Routledge.

Lewis, J. and Davies, K. (2004) *Literacy and Numeracy Staff Handbook for Use in Approved Premises*. Ellsmere: Be Consultancy.

Lewis, S., McGuire, M., Raynor, P., Vanstone, M., Vennard, J. (2003) *The Resettlement of Short Term Prisoners: Evaluation of Seven Pathfinders. Research Findings 200* London: Home Office.

Loney, K., Peaden, A., Wallace, J. and Stephens, K. (2000) *Pro-social Modelling: Report on Implementation in Hostel*. London: National Probation Service.

Lunness, T. (2000) Smart thinking: social and moral reasoning with young people – stop to think or think to stop. *Youth Justice Matters*, March 2000 8–10.

Mair, G. (ed.) (2004) *What Matters in Probation*. Devon: Willan.

Macpherson, W. (1999) *The Stephen Lawrence Inquiry*. London: The Stationery Office.

Manzoor, S. (2005) *Don't Call Me Asian*, Radio 4, see also *We've Ditched Race for Religion*, Guardian.

Maruna, S. (2000) Desistance from crime and offender rehabilitation: A tale of two research literatures. *Offender Programmes Report* 4, 5–9.

Mehabrian, A. (1972) *Non-verbal Communication*. Chicago: Aldine Atherstone.

McConville, S. (2003) *The Uses of Punishment*. Devon: Willan.

McGuire, J. and Priestley, P. (1985) *Offending Behaviour, Skills and Stratagems for Going Straight*. London: Batsford.

McGuire, J. (2000) *Cognitive Behavioural Approaches: An Introduction to Theory and Research*. London: HM Inspectorate of Probation.

McIvor, G. (1998) Pro-social modelling and legitimacy: lessons from a study of community service, in Rex and Maltravers (1998) *op. cit.*

McIvor, G. and Barry, M. (2000) *Social Work and Criminal Justice: Volume 8 – The Longer-term Effectiveness of Supervision*. Edinburgh: Scottish Executive Central Research Unit.

McNeil, F. (2003) Desistance focussed probation practice, in Chui and Nellis *op. cit.*

Miller, W.R. and Rollnick, S. (1991) *Motivational Interviewing – Preparing People to Change Addictive Behaviours*. New York: Guildford.

Miller, W. and Rollnick, S. (2002) *Motivational Interviewing*. New York: Guildford.

183

Morris, B. (2004) *The Case for Change: People in the Metropolitan Police Service.* London: The Morris Enquiry.

National Literary Trust (2004) Accessed from: www.literacytrust.org.uk/ socialinclusion/index.html

NOMS (2005) The NOMs Offender Management Model Version 1 Internal Paper.

NUT (2004) Averted-eyed children more intelligent. Accessed from: http://www. teachers.org.uk/showwirearchive.php?id=1924571 Report on forthcoming research.

O'Connell, B. (1998) *Solution Focussed Therapy.* London: Sage.

PA Consultancy Group and MORI (2005) Action Research Study of the National Offender Management Model in the North West. Home Office Online Rep no. 32/05. London.

Player, E. and Jenkins, M. (1993) *Prisons After Woolf: Reform through Riot.* Oxford: Routledge.

Rex, S. and Maltravers, A. (1998) *Pro-social Modelling and Legitimacy; The Clarke Hall Day Conference Institute of Criminology.* Cambridge: Cambridge University Press.

Rex, S. (1999) Desistance from offending: experiences of probation. *Howard Journal of Criminal Justice* 38: 366–383.

Rex, S.A. and Crosland, P.E. (1999) *Project on pro-social modelling and legitimacy: findings from community service.* Cambridge University: Institute of Criminology.

Rex, S. (2004) Beyond cognitive behaviourism? Reflections on the effectiveness literature, in Bottoms *et. al. op. cit.*

Rex, S., Gelsthorpe, L., Roberts, C. and Jordan, P. (2004) *A process and outcome evaluation of community service pathfinder projects. Home Office Occasional Paper No 87.* London: Home Office.

Rogers, C.R. (1951) *Client Centred Therapy.* Boston: Houghton-Mifflin.

Rose, M.P. (1990) Barriers to equality: the power of subtle discrimination to maintain unequal opportunity. *Employee Responsibility and Rights Journal,* 3(2), 153–163.

Ruxton, S. (2003) *Men, Masculinities and Poverty in the UK:* Oxford: Oxfam Publishing.

Sinclair, I. (1971) *Hostels for Probationers: A Study of the Aims, Working and Variations in Effectiveness of Male Probation Hostels with Special Reference to the Influence of Environment on Delinquency. Home Office Research Studies, No. 6.* London: HMSO.

Smith, David (2003) *The Edinburgh Study of Youth Transitions and Crime.* London: Economic and Social Research Council.

Sumerel, M.B. (1994) *Parallel Processes in Supervision.* ERIC Clearing House on Counselling and Student Services.

Trotter, C. (1994) *The Effective Supervision of Offenders: A Training Manual.* Melbourne, Australia: Victoria Department of Justice and the Monash University Social Work.

Trotter, C. (1999) *Working with Involuntary Clients.* Sage: London.

Trotter, C. (2000) Social work education, pro-social modelling and effective probation practice. *Probation Journal,* 47: 256–261.

Trotter, C. (2004) *Helping Abused Children and their Families; Towards an Evidence Based Treatment Model.* London: Sage.

Tuklo Orenda Associates (1999) *Making a Difference.* Bridgewater: South West Probation Training Consortium.

Woolf, H. and Tumin, S. (1991) *Prison Disturbances April 1990, Cm 1456.* London: Home Office.

Willis, L. and Daisley, J. (1995) *The Assertive Trainer.* London: McGraw Hill.

YJB (2000) *Use of Rewards and Incentives in Work With Young People in Secure Accommodation.* London: Youth Justice Board.

Index